AMY'S PROMISE AN
BROWNIE STORIES

Ever since she could remember, Amy had wanted to be a Brownie. On her seventh birthday she was excited because being seven meant moving up from Rainbows.

When Amy had learned everything she needed to know to make her Promise and become a real Brownie, her mum took her to the Guide Shop in town and bought her uniform. Back home, Amy put it on and admired herself in the mirror.

The day of Amy's Promise Ceremony drew near. Amy practised her Law and Promise, so that she would say it perfectly and marked off the days on the calendar.

The night before the great day, Amy was very jumpy. She couldn't keep still. And that was the cause of the disaster . . .

Amy's Promise and Other Brownie Stories

by various authors

KNIGHT BOOKS
Hodder and Stoughton

First published in Great Britain in this collection by Knight Books in 1992

All these stories have previously appeared in the *Brownie* magazine. The Girl Guides Association has made every reasonable attempt to contact the authors involved. However, if anyone has been overlooked, the Girl Guides Association will seek to make amends.

A CIP catalogue record for this title is available from the British Library

ISBN 0-340-58002-X

The characters and situations in this book are entirely imaginary and bear no relation to any real person or actual happenings.

Printed and bound in Great Britain for Hodder and Stoughton Children's Books a division of Hodder and Stoughton Ltd., Mill Road, Dunton Green, Sevenoaks, Kent TN13 2YA. (Editorial Office: 47 Bedford Square, London WC1B 3DP) by Clays Ltd, St Ives plc. Photoset by Rowland Phototypesetting Ltd., Bury St Edmunds, Suffolk.

Contents

1 Amy's Promise *Gillian Ellis* 7
2 Tin Cans and Lampshades *Janet Chamberlain* 14
3 The Tea Party *Janet Chamberlain* 21
4 Moving Day *Anne Forsyth* 28
5 Balloon Message *Ailsa Brambleby* 34
6 Bruno Makes Amends *Catherine Courtney* 44
7 Hannah Helps Out *Anne Forsyth* 51
8 The Almond Present *Nancy Scott* 57
9 A Challenge from Uncle Bill *Ailsa Brambleby* 62
10 Jenny's Christmas Present *Judy F. Taylor* 73
11 Pippa of the Pixies *Gillian Ellis* 80
12 The Chickenpox Camp *Sheila Norton* 86
13 Get Well Soon *Anne Forsyth* 93
14 Christmas Just As It Should Be *Jean Hilton* 99
15 Pennies for Our Thoughts *Ailsa Brambleby* 104

16 Castle Adventure *Lynn Hurdwell* 115

17 Beccy Wins Through *Judy F. Taylor* 122

18 The Unexpected Bridesmaid *Diane Chorley* 128

19 Fat Fred *Gillian Ellis* 134

20 The Brownie Who Was Scared of the Dark *Gillian Ellis* 142

21 Just a Piece of String *Ailsa Brambleby* 149

Amy's Promise

Ever since she could remember, Amy had wanted to be a Brownie. On her seventh birthday she was excited because being seven meant moving up from Rainbows. Rainbows had been fun, but Amy thought Brownies would be even better.

Brown Owl put Amy in the Elves. The Sixer was called Joanne and she was really nice. She showed Amy how everything was done and told her the Law and Promise, then chose her as a partner for games.

Soon Amy had learned everything she needed to know to make her Promise and become a real Brownie, so her mum took her to the Guide Shop in town and bought her uniform. Back home, Amy put it on and admired herself in the mirror.

'It's lovely!' she said, happily. 'Thank you, Mum! It'll be easy to be a real Brownie with my nice new uniform to remind me!'

The day of Amy's Promise Ceremony drew

near. Amy practised her Law and Promise, so that she would say it perfectly, and marked off the days on the calendar.

The night before the great day, Amy was very jumpy. She couldn't keep still. At bath-time she danced upstairs singing 'Happy Promise to me, Happy Promise to me! Happy Promise, dear Amy, Happy Promise to me!' at the top of her voice till everyone begged her to stop. Amy's mum helped her out of the bath and smiled at the excited face.

'Calm down,' she said, wrapping Amy in a bath-towel. 'You'll never get to sleep tonight!' But Amy just giggled and began to hop around the bathroom. When her mother tried to catch her, she darted away, still wrapped in the towel.

And that was the cause of the disaster. As Amy hopped along the landing, her foot caught in the towel and, before she could grab the bannister to save herself, she fell headlong down the stairs.

Her father's voice sounded far away as though he spoke through cotton wool. Amy slowly opened her eyes to see her mother's face floating above her. Her eyes were blurred and her head hurt. She peered around hazily and found she was lying on the settee covered with a blanket. Her father was speaking on the telephone. Amy

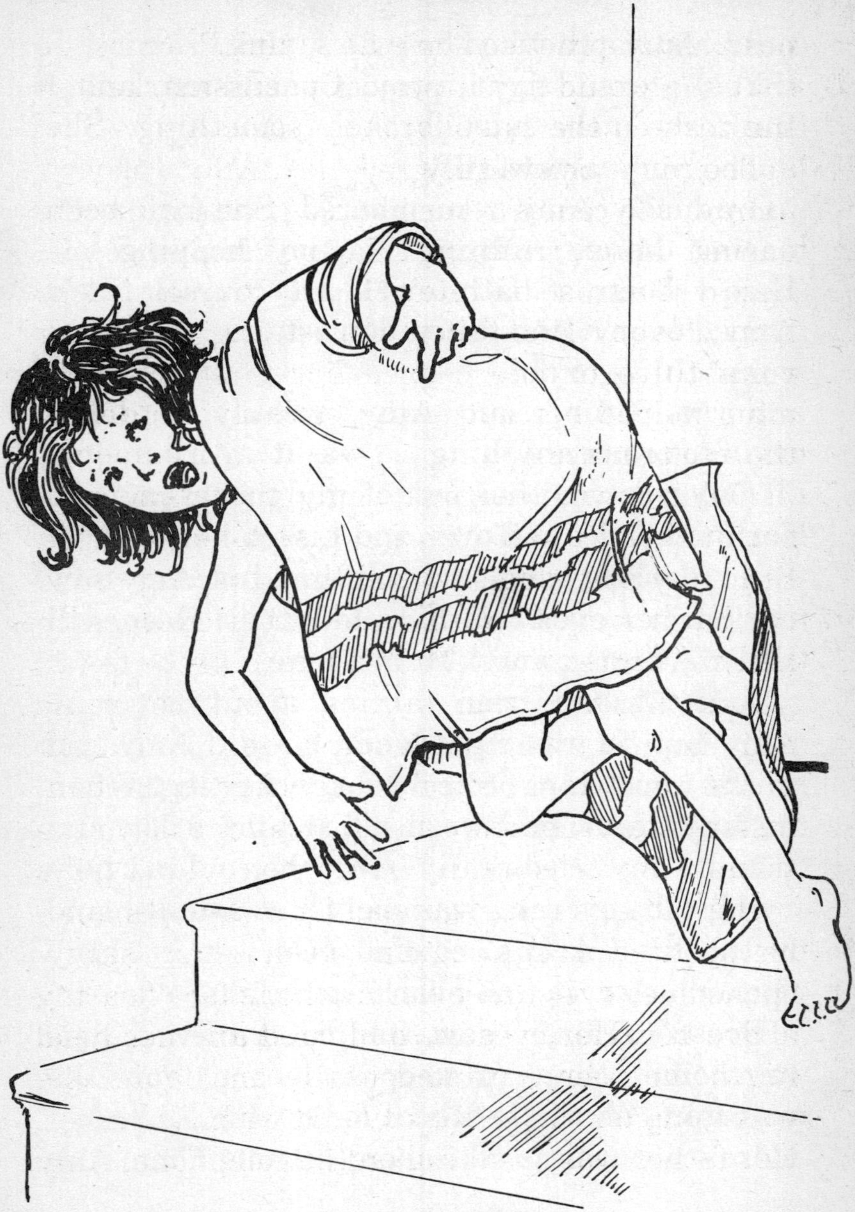

could just catch what he was saying.

'Yes, please, right away. Concussion, and I think she may have broken something. She landed very awkwardly . . .'

Gradually Amy remembered. She had been teasing Mum, running . . . no, hopping . . . there'd been a bath-towel. Of course! She'd tripped over it and fallen downstairs . . . what a stupid thing to do!

'Sorry, Mum,' said Amy, weakly. 'I didn't mean to break anything . . . was it an ornament? I'll buy you another out of my pocket-money.' Her mother leaned over and kissed her.

'No, darling,' she said, smiling, but Amy saw tears in her eyes. 'Nothing like that. Keep still till Dr Adams comes. Mum's here.'

Daddy hadn't been talking about an ornament, but he was right when he said Amy had broken something. She'd broken her leg. When the first shock had worn off, it hurt a lot, and though Amy tried really hard, she couldn't help crying. The evening was spent in Casualty, and by the time Amy's leg had been set in shiny white plaster, it was nearly midnight.

'Doesn't matter,' said Dad cheerfully, on the way home. 'You can sleep as long as you like tomorrow, Amy. No school for a while.'

Amy was sorry. She liked school. Then suddenly her heart lurched – tomorrow was Thursday!

'Oh no!' she gasped, 'my Brownie Promise!'

'Another time,' said her mother, hugging her, but Amy was heartbroken. She had counted the days for so long.

Amy couldn't sleep that night, partly because her leg hurt, but mainly because she was upset. The Promise Ceremony danced before her eyes. What a terrible disappointment!

Her mother tried to keep her occupied next day, but Amy wasn't interested. She longed to go to Brownies, but her mum was firm.

'You need rest,' she said, and went to phone Brown Owl with the news. She talked a long time and came back looking pleased.

'Brown Owl says she'll pop round after Brownies tonight and you can make your Promise here.' Amy felt better instantly.

'It won't be the same,' she said. 'But it's better than nothing.'

After tea, Amy's mum helped her to put on her uniform.

'May as well look the part,' she said, smiling. Amy watched the clock, wishing she could be with the others.

Suddenly the door burst open and in poured all the Brownies!

'We've come for the Promise Ceremony!' said Joanne, grinning at Amy's face. 'Your mum invited the whole Pack and the other mums and dads!'

'It'll be a squash,' grinned Amy's dad. 'But different!'

It was! Both a squash and different but Amy loved every minute! After the ceremony, Amy's mum brought orange juice and cake and the Brownies sang funny songs. Then Brown Owl hugged Amy and everyone went home.

‘Oh, Mum!’ said Amy, eyes shining. ‘You’re the best in the world! How can I thank you enough?’

‘Just don’t play near the stairs again!’ said her father.

‘I promise,’ said Amy, for the second time that evening.

GILLIAN ELLIS

Tin Cans and Lampshades

One Saturday afternoon, Sally's father was tidying out his shed.

'I don't know where all this rubbish comes from,' he said. 'Most of this stuff belongs in the bin.'

'What about this?' said Sally, holding up a lampshade. 'Do you want me to save it?'

Dad shook his head. 'No – put it on the rubbish pile,' he told her, 'and those empty plastic bottles can go out as well.'

Sally bent down to pick them up. 'There's a big sack of straw down here,' she called out. 'You must have bought it when we had the rabbit.'

'There's no point in hanging on to that,' Dad answered. 'I'll put it by the bin.'

Just at that moment, Sally's big brothers, Ben and Peter, came racing up the drive.

'Cor, look at this lot!' shouted Ben, eyeing the rubbish.

'There's some wood here!' yelled Pete.

'You boys can have that,' Dad told them. 'Go in the shed and I'll show you how to make some model boats.'

'Can I have a boat too?' cried Sally. 'I've never done any woodwork.'

'Girls don't do woodwork,' said Ben, pushing past her.

'Girls *can't* do woodwork,' added Pete.

'Look, Sal,' said Dad lifting down his toolbox. 'You're a bit small for this sort of thing, so why don't you go back in the house and help Mum with the washing up? It can be your good deed for the day.'

'Brownies don't always do housework,' Sally said indignantly. 'We can do lots of other things as well.'

Pete ran inside the shed. 'Yes, but woodwork isn't one of them,' he replied, closing the door.

Sally went into the kitchen. 'Would you like me to wash up?' she asked her mother.

'Not yet,' Mum said. 'I've run out of washing-up liquid. Would you slip down to the shop and get me some?'

When Sally reached the shop, Mr Goodacre, the grocer, was deep in conversation with the vicar.

'How's your garden coming along?' Mr Good-

acre was saying. 'I saw you out there the other afternoon.'

'Not very well I'm afraid,' the vicar replied. 'The birds keep attacking my plants.'

'You'll have to make a scarecrow,' Mr Goodacre told him. 'That'll keep them away.'

'Easier said than done,' the vicar sighed, and with his mind still fixed firmly on his garden, he walked sadly out of the door.

'Now, Sally, what can I get you?' Mr Goodacre asked.

But Sally was staring down the street. 'I think I might be able to help the vicar,' she told him.

Back home in Sally's garden, the shed door remained very firmly closed. From inside there came the sound of banging and hammering, but Sally didn't mind.

Next to the rubbish heap was a packet of bin bags. Sally took one out and filled it with plastic bottles. Then she picked up the broom handle and placed it across a long piece of wood.

'Oh dear, I need a nail,' she sighed, and knocked loudly on the shed door.

'What do you want?' Pete yelled, jerking it open. 'And whatever's that?'

'I'm making a present for the vicar,' Sally said loftily. 'And I need a hammer and nail.'

'Did you hear that?' Pete sniggered. 'Our

Sally's making a present for the vicar! I don't know what it's going to be – but she's using two bits of wood and a polythene bag!'

'Don't be unkind,' Dad told him. 'She can have that little hammer over there.'

The hammer was passed over along with some nails. 'I bet you wish you were doing woodwork,' Pete whispered, and closed the door in her face.

Sally went back into the kitchen. 'Here's your washing-up liquid,' she said to her mum. 'And please could you find me some old clothes?'

Mum raised her eyebrows in surprise. 'There's a bag of jumble in the cupboard,' she told her.

Sally picked out an old overcoat of her father's and some trousers and trainers.

'Do you need them for anything special?' Mum enquired.

Sally nodded. 'I'm making the vicar a scarecrow,' she whispered.

'Tell you what,' Mum said kindly, 'I'll give you a hand.'

With Mum's help the scarecrow soon began to take shape. 'It needs a head now!' Mum exclaimed. 'What can we use for that?'

Sally had a rummage in the junk pile. 'We'll use this old football,' she decided. 'With a lampshade for a hat!'

'It's looking really good now,' Mum said a little

while later. 'Is there anything else you need?'

'Well, I'd like it to bang and rattle,' Sally said thoughtfully, 'but I haven't got anything that makes a noise.'

Mum disappeared into the kitchen and came out carrying some empty drink cans. 'How about these?' she smiled. 'We could hang them on bits of string.'

Suddenly the shed door flew open. 'Any chance

of a drink?' Dad began. Then he stopped, and he stared, and he smiled.

'Our Sally's made a scarecrow!' he called out over his shoulder. 'Come and have a look!'

'Wow!' said Pete. 'That's really good!'

'I wish I could make one,' said Ben. 'It looks much more fun than model boats.'

'Well,' Mum said brightly, 'perhaps we can do a deal. If Dad would like to help Sally with some woodwork, then I might be able to find enough bits and pieces to make a couple more scarecrows.'

'Yes!' cried Ben and Pete together.

By the end of the afternoon, three strange-looking characters were standing guard over the vicar's vegetables. They had bodies made of straw, plastic bottles, and goodness knows what.

'Your scarecrows have really made my day,' the vicar told Sally and her brothers. 'I've been feeling a bit down in the dumps just lately, but now – I'm full of beans!'

'As long as the birds aren't!' Sally laughed.

JANET CHAMBERLAIN

The Tea Party

'It's perfect,' said Mum.

'Yes,' agreed Kelly as she carefully lifted the sponge cake out of the oven. It really was perfect. It was golden brown and smelt delicious.

'I'll put some raspberry jam in the middle and a little icing sugar on top,' Kelly said thoughtfully. 'Oh Mum, do you think I'll pass my Hostess badge?'

'Of course I do,' said her mother. 'But you've still got plenty to do if you're going to be ready by four o'clock.'

Kelly had wanted to take her Hostess badge for a long time and had been wondering who she could invite to tea. Then, one day, she had a wonderful idea.

'Mrs Robinson who lives at number 20! I don't think she goes out much. Perhaps she would like to come to tea. I'll ask Brown Owl if someone can come and test me.'

At the next Brownie meeting, Brown Owl told

Kelly that Mrs Robinson could be her tester. 'It seems that the District Commissioner knows Mrs Robinson quite well. Her daughter is a Guider too. She told me that Mrs Robinson used to be a cookery teacher.'

'Oh dear,' said Kelly. 'I hope she won't be too strict.'

Brown Owl laughed, 'You will certainly need to try very hard. Remember you have to write an invitation as well.'

Kelly wrote the invitation out three times before she was satisfied with it. Then, when she was sure it was really neat and that all the words were spelt correctly, she posted it through Mrs Robinson's letter box.

She didn't have to wait very long for a reply. That afternoon, when she came home from school, the answer was waiting for her.

Mrs Robinson thanked her for her kind invitation and said she would be delighted to come to tea on Saturday.

Now Saturday had come. The morning seemed to fly by. Even Frisky, the puppy, seemed to realise something exciting was happening as he scampered about, licking up crumbs from the floor.

'I'm sorry about the crumbs, Mum,' said Kelly. 'But at least Frisky is enjoying them.'

'I don't think they're good for him,' replied Mum. 'He had better go out of the kitchen while you're preparing the food. Mind you don't trip over him when you carry those sandwiches. It would be a shame if you dropped them after all your hard work.'

Kelly began to lay the table. She covered it with a clean tablecloth and set out the best china. The sandwiches were carefully arranged and covered with clingfilm, ready to be uncovered when Kelly's guest arrived. In the centre of the table went the best thing of all, Kelly's beautiful sponge cake with a glistening coat of icing sugar.

Kelly looked at the table carefully. There was something missing. 'Of course, a flower arrangement,' said Kelly and ran off into the garden to collect some flowers.

She returned a quarter of an hour later to put the flowers on the table. As she entered the dining room she stopped and gave a shout.

For there, sitting in the centre of the carefully laid table, was Frisky, contentedly licking the icing sugar off the top of Kelly's lovely cake! And Mrs Robinson was due to arrive in a quarter of an hour!

'Oh Mum!' wailed Kelly. 'What am I going to do now? Frisky has ruined everything.'

'Oh dear,' said Kelly's mum, 'what a mess!' She looked at the table with horror.

'There's nothing I can do now, Mum,' said Kelly, almost in tears. 'Mrs Robinson will be here in fifteen minutes.'

'There must be something you can do,' said Mum. 'Surely there is something you can make in a quarter of an hour. After all, the sandwiches are still all right. Frisky hasn't touched them.'

'No, he's definitely got a sweet tooth,' said Kelly with a weak smile. Then she had an idea.

'Mum, I could make some of those chocolate cornflake cakes you made for my last party. They only take a few minutes to make. They could set while I entertained Mrs Robinson.'

'That's a good idea,' agreed Mum. 'But you'll still have to do something about the table. Frisky's left footprints all over the cloth.'

Kelly thought for a while.

'We'll have tea in the garden,' she decided. 'It's a nice day and quite warm enough.'

While her mother shut Frisky in another room, Kelly began making her new batch of cakes. Of course, they weren't as nice as her lovely sponge cake, but they looked really delicious.

Soon Mrs Robinson arrived and sat down to tea in the garden with Kelly and her mother.

'I have enjoyed myself this afternoon,' said Mrs Robinson after tea. 'The tea was delicious and your garden is so pretty.'

Kelly sighed with relief. Everything had turned out well after all.

'You must come to tea more often,' Kelly's mother said.

'That's kind of you. You are all so friendly, even your little dog.' She stroked Frisky's ears. 'He is sweet, isn't he?'

Kelly agreed. 'Yes, he is, but I'm afraid he's been very naughty this afternoon.' And she told Mrs Robinson all that had happened.

How the old lady laughed! 'What a shame, after all your hard work. Still, those chocolate cakes were lovely. You must give me the recipe. My granddaughter is coming to stay during the holidays and I'm sure she would love them.'

Then she had an idea. 'I know, why don't you come over one day and show us how to make them? Then you can stay to tea and help us to eat them as well. My granddaughter is about your age, I'm sure you'll get on well together.'

'I'd love to,' said Kelly. 'I'm so glad everything turned out well. Perhaps I should thank Frisky. If he hadn't eaten the cake, then I wouldn't have made those others and found a new friend.'

JANET CHAMBERLAIN

Moving Day

Moving house! Mandy was very excited. A new house and a garden with a swing! She'd be going to a new school too. Of course, she wouldn't feel too strange because she would soon make some new friends. And hopefully she'd be able to join a new Brownie Pack right away.

Mandy was a little sad to be leaving all her friends in her old Pack. 'Goodbye, we'll miss you!' they had all said, as they gave her a huge card signed by all the Brownies.

'I won't be at rehearsals,' thought Mandy. The Pack were doing a pantomime – *Dick Whittington* – this year and Mandy had been looking forward to playing the part of the cat. She wouldn't be joining in the sponsored silence either or going to visit the Guide Dog Training Centre.

What a lot she was going to miss. Then she remembered that Brownies are always cheerful and started to wonder what exciting things she'd be doing with her new Pack: Brownie revels, Pack Holiday, outings, badge work and lots, lots more.

But right now she was far too busy to think about days or weeks ahead, because today was moving day.

'Won't be long now,' said Mum. The removal van would be arriving any minute. Dad had already gone on ahead to the new house.

Soon the men would load all the furniture into the van – beds, chairs, tables, boxes of china, pots and pans and clothes and books and lots of other things.

Now the house looked very bare. All the rooms were huge and empty and there were marks on the walls where the pictures had hung.

'Can I help?' Mandy asked her mother.

Mum looked round the kitchen. Everything was ready to be moved. For weeks the family had been sorting out, tidying up and taking rubbish to the dump.

'I don't think there's anything left to do,' said Mum.

Just then Ben, the baby, started to cry. His face got redder and redder and his wails got louder.

'What's the matter?' Mum picked him up. He didn't seem to be wet or cold or hungry.

FRAGILE
HANDLE
WITH CARE
FRAGILE
HANDLE
WITH CARE

‘Perhaps he’s bored,’ said Mandy.

‘All his toys have been packed – I know that,’ said Mum.

‘Maybe he wants a spoon to play with.’ Mandy knew that her little brother liked to bang a spoon against his tray.

‘They’re packed too,’ said Mum.

‘Come on, Ben, we’ll play a game,’ said Mandy.

‘Oh thanks,’ said Mum. ‘It would be a great help if you could keep him happy for a little while.’

Mandy and Ben went into Mandy’s bedroom. The room was as empty as all the other rooms. No books, no pictures, no games, no toys.

First Mandy tried telling her little brother a story. But he didn’t want to listen. Then she tried finger games, but that wasn’t any good either. She tried singing to him, but Ben just kept on crying.

‘You don’t like all this fuss and upheaval, do you?’ she said.

Then she noticed a pile of newspapers in the corner of the room. They had been used for packing. They gave Mandy an idea.

‘Look, Ben!’ She took a page from one of the newspapers and folded it in half. She tore a semicircle out of the fold and opened the paper again. There was a big circle. She peeped through it.

'Boo!' The baby suddenly stopped crying and smiled.

Mandy had another idea. She folded the paper in half, then in half again and then from corner to corner. Then she tore little holes in the fold. It would have been easier with scissors, but they were packed away in a box somewhere.

She shook out the paper. 'What's this, Ben?'

It was a fancy mat full of holes.

The baby laughed and grabbed the paper.

Next, Mandy made a fan by folding a strip of paper. She gave it to Ben to wave.

Then she made a strip of dancing dolls all holding hands.

Every time Mandy made something new she handed it to Ben, who started tearing the paper up. He was chuckling and smiling now.

'It's very quiet in here,' said Mum, popping her head round the door. 'Paper tearing, what a good idea!'

The baby waved a paper mat at her.

Mum laughed.

'It's a bit untidy,' said Mandy, looking round at all the paper. The room certainly did look untidy, with little bits of paper like confetti everywhere. She remembered that Brownies always clear up. 'I'll just get the pan and brush,' she said.

'I know where they are. I haven't packed them yet,' said Mum. 'Thank you, Mandy. Two good turns in one! And the van's just arrived so we'll soon be off.'

ANNE FORSYTH

Balloon Message

As Ann stood gazing at the balloons at the Hospital Fête, an idea jumped into her head. Immediately a quiver of excitement, like a trickle of silver, ran through her body. She always felt like this when she had a new idea, especially if it was a good one; and this one wasn't just good – it was super!

Ann eased herself through the crowds until she was right up by the balloon stall. She would need to understand exactly what happened there to make sure that her plan would work.

She watched the young medical student blow up a balloon from a cylinder of special gas. He handed this to a customer who wrote his name and address on a label and tied it to the balloon which he then released.

'Come on, have a go!' called the student. 'Only ten pence a turn and we'll see whose balloon is sent back from the farthest place. A prize for the winner!'

‘Please,’ asked Ann, ‘could they go to France?’

‘Sure thing.’

‘What about Italy or Switzerland?’

‘No problem. France, Italy, Switzerland, Germany, Spain . . . probably Timbuktu and the North Pole.’

‘Thank you, but I don’t want Timbuktu or the North Pole.’

‘Well, have a go anyway.’

‘I’m not ready yet. What time do you close your stall?’

‘Not until the fête closes at six – unless we’re sold out before then.’

‘Oh dear, and it’s half past four already,’ said Ann. ‘That doesn’t give me much time.’

‘Funny kid,’ laughed the student as Ann ran off. ‘Come on, you folks, only ten pence a go!’

Ann hurried over to the other side of the field and through a gate which led into her own back garden.

‘My word! You’re back soon,’ exclaimed her mother. ‘Didn’t you find any friends to talk to?’

‘Mum, you *know* I haven’t any friends here – not yet,’ said Ann impatiently.

‘No, dear, I suppose it is difficult. It’s a pity we had to move just at the beginning of the holidays; but never mind, you’ll have plenty of friends when school starts.’

'I'm not all that sure that I shall,' replied Ann, gloomily. 'It seems a funny place to me, not having a Brownie Pack, and I expect it'll be a funny sort of school too.'

'Nonsense, dear,' said her mother with a laugh, but she felt sorry for Ann who was certainly lonely.

Ann brightened suddenly as she remembered her idea.

'Mum, d'you mind if I go down to the shops a minute?'

'Well all right, as long as you only go into the shops we've been in together.'

'Good!' Ann ran into her room for a pencil and note book and then hurried to Madame Perren's café. In the window were the most mouth-watering cream cakes, and inside, the walls were covered with scenes of Switzerland, cow bells and a large cuckoo clock.

'Great! Not many customers,' thought Ann as she walked up to Madame Perren who was sitting regally in her black silk dress behind the counter.

'Please,' said Ann, 'I've heard that you're very good at languages . . .'

'Ah well, my child, not so very good, but we Swiss, we speak ze German, and we learn a leetle French and a leetle Italian, yes.'

'Germany, France, Italy and Switzerland. Oh that's marvellous! Please, Madame Perren, will you help me, please?'

'But of course, if I can.' Madame Perren listened carefully, nodding her head and smiling as she learned Ann's plan.

'Yes, yes,' she said. 'I can help.' She took Ann's note book and wrote down some words in it, and then she said, 'I too have an idea. Why not Danish?'

'But I don't know anyone from Denmark.'

'Ah, but I do. Ze new young lady at the swimming bath, Margrethe she is called. She comes from Denmark to learn English.'

'Smashing!' exclaimed Ann. 'I know who you mean. Mummy pointed her out to me last time we were at the baths.'

'Oh but it's no good,' she added, disappointed. 'It's twenty pence to go into the baths as a spectator and I've got to keep ten pence for the balloon and I shall need some money to get into the fête again!'

'Ah, child, no bother. I have many good friends in Denmark. You have the money from me in memory of my friends!'

The bell of the till rang and the next minute Ann had a twenty pence piece in her hand.

'Oh thank you, thank you!' she cried and ran

out of the café just as the cuckoo clock was striking five. 'Oh dear, half an hour gone already.'

Ann rushed to the baths, paid her entrance fee, then walked along by the spectators' benches until she saw the tall fair-haired Margrethe.

'Oh help,' said Ann to herself. 'She seems to have dozens of pupils.'

Impatiently she waited, looking alternately at the clock and at the instructress. At last she could speak to her, but oh dear, how slow she was to understand! 'I'll explain just once more,' thought Ann, 'and if she doesn't get it this time, I'll have to leave it!'

'Oh ja, ja, ja!' came the answer at last. 'I see, I see!' Quickly she added something to Ann's note book.

'Five. That should be enough,' said Ann with satisfaction. 'And I've just enough time left.'

Then she hurried back to the fête.

She bought her balloon and then went off to a quiet corner to write the label – but not just her name and address. Those she put in small letters, then using the correct foreign words given to her by Madame Perren and Margrethe she wrote:

'If found in France, please give to a Jeannette.

If found in Switzerland, please give to a Little Bee.
If found in Germany, please give to a Wichtel.
If found in Italy, please give to a Coccinella.
If found in Denmark, please give to a Grønsmutte.'

She walked to the middle of the field, waited for a breeze and tossed up her balloon. She watched it till it disappeared over the trees and then she ran home.

'And if that doesn't bring me a Brownie pen-friend, I don't know what will!' she exclaimed after she had told the whole story to her mother.

That night, Ann's last thought was of her balloon, high above the clouds, floating away over the seas to find her a Brownie pen-friend. She fell asleep, a smile on her face.

There would have been no smile if she had seen the short and ill-fated journey of her balloon. It had risen jauntily into the breeze in the hospital field, but no sooner had it reached the gardens bordering it, than the wind dropped, the balloon sank a little, caught in a tree, burst, and hung there, a poor tattered scrap of rubber with a crumpled label attached.

Ann spent so much time indoors waiting for the postman that her mother was quite glad

FETE

when her daughter was invited to stay with cousins for a few days.

'Any news, Mum? Any news of the balloon?' were Ann's first words on her return.

'Well no, I'm afraid not – but there are two other bits of news for you. First, our new neighbours have arrived: they moved in while you were away, and second, there's a letter for you.'

'From abroad?'

'No, darling. Sorry.'

Disappointed, Ann slit open the envelope.

'Mum, you're wrong! It *is* from abroad. Listen:

"Dear Ann,

I am not a Jeannette of France, a Little Bee of Switzerland, a Wichtel of Germany, a Coccinella of Italy, or a Grønsmutte of Denmark, but I *am* a Bulbul of India, so please will I do as your pen-friend?"

'Mummy, just think! My balloon got all the way to India!'

'But, Ann, it couldn't have. Let me see. What's the address on the letter?'

'Thirty-five Edward Street,' read Ann, 'But that's impossible. *This* is Edward Street.'

'And we're thirty-seven,' said Ann's mother, just as mystified as her daughter. 'Is there anything more in the letter?'

Ann turned it over. 'Yes, there is.' She read on:

> 'Do you like climbing trees? I do, and I was thrilled to see the large tree in this garden when we moved here and I climbed it straight away and that's when I found your letter . . .

'My letter? My balloon in that tree all the time? But, Mum, it can't be true because she says she's a Bulbul from India.'

'Oh yes it can be true! I've not seen your Bulbul yet, but I *have* seen her father: he's the new doctor at the hospital, an Indian one, just arrived from India.'

Ann clapped her hands in delight.

'I knew my idea would work – but it's even better still. I thought it would bring me a pen-friend, but it's brought me a real Brownie friend instead!'

AILSA BRAMBLEBY

Bruno Makes Amends

'Bruno, get down,' laughed Helen, fending off her puppy's friendly licks. 'You can play all you want when we get to the park.' She slipped a lead over his head. 'You will have to go to bed early tonight though,' she added thoughtfully. 'It's Bonfire Night and I don't want you to be frightened by all those sparks and bangs.'

Helen's mother smiled. 'Soon you'll be able to take Bruno to obedience classes,' she remarked. 'That will be good for him and it should please Mrs Johnson next door.'

Helen sighed. Because she was a Brownie she tried hard to be kind and helpful but recently she and Bruno seemed only to have upset their elderly neighbour.

In August, Bruno had hardly been hers for a week when he decided to explore the garden. Unseen, he had squeezed through a gap into Mrs Johnson's garden. There he discovered a tortoise nibbling on the grass. Bruno's wild barks

brought the old lady out of the house, waving a stick, and Helen was called to take her puppy away in disgrace.

'Freddie is my granddaughter's tortoise,' explained Mrs Johnson. 'She is abroad for a few months and I agreed to have it while she is away. I can't allow it to be frightened by your dog. If something happened to it I couldn't even replace it – you can't buy tortoises in pet shops any more. Imagine how I would feel!'

Helen and her parents nodded apologetically and promised that it would not happen again.

Since then their neighbour had been poorly. 'I am really very sorry to mention it,' she said one day, 'but is it possible to keep Bruno a little quieter? I do need as much rest as I can get and that little chap does seem to be particularly noisy.'

Helen was miserable. 'What can I do?' she asked. 'I don't want to spoil Mrs Johnson's rest but I can't stop Bruno from barking sometimes. He is only a puppy.'

Her mother was just as worried. She and Mrs Johnson had been good neighbours for years, something she did not want to change.

In the park the November leaves speckled the ground. Bruno bounded happily through the long grass while Helen and her mother collected sticks for a bonfire. It was to be a really magnificent one decided Helen, who had asked her friend Louise to come and share the fun that evening. Suddenly she had an idea. 'Mummy, do you think we should tell Mrs Johnson about our fireworks?' she suggested. 'Louise says her gran loves them.'

'That's a lovely idea, Helen,' agreed her mother. 'She might like to come and watch the bonfire. I sometimes think she must get rather lonely all on her own. Bruno will be safely tucked up in the house. It might be a way of saying sorry for having disturbed her a bit recently. Why don't you pop round as soon as we get back and ask her?'

Mrs Johnson was out when Helen called. 'Never mind,' said her mother, 'you can ask her later. How about helping me in the kitchen for a while?'

They prepared baked potatoes, apples and sausages. As the cooking smells filled the kitchen Bruno appeared round the door, his tail wagging hopefully. Helen jumped up. 'Come on. One more run round the garden and then I'm going to put you in your basket. Dad will be lighting the bonfire soon and I can hear Louise.'

She let Bruno into the garden. He ran towards the bonfire, thrust his nose at the pile of sticks and began to bark furiously. 'I had better fetch him inside before he disturbs the whole neighbourhood,' said Helen as she answered the door to Louise.

'Hang on,' said Louise, watching with interest while Bruno rushed excitedly at the branches, waving his tail frantically from side to side. 'I think he's found something.'

Helen's parents came up to see what all the noise was. Her father pulled Bruno out of the

way and shone his torch into the pile of sticks. 'Nothing here,' he said, 'only leaves and twigs and . . . good heavens, there is something . . . It's a tortoise!' Gently he lifted the little animal out. It was quite still. He examined the creature closely. 'I think it's hibernating. Though what it is doing in our bonfire, I can't imagine. I suppose we had better take it next door and ask Mrs Johnson if it is hers.'

The old lady was astonished. 'What a discovery!' she exclaimed. 'But it can't be Freddie. I tucked him up in his winter box only yesterday. He was practically asleep. Look, I'll show you.'

They all went to the garden shed. A cardboard carton was lying on its side, straw spilling everywhere. Mrs Johnson gave a little gasp. Helen's father laughed, 'It seems that Freddie wasn't so sleepy after all. He must have crawled out and started exploring. By the time he really was ready to hibernate he had reached our bonfire. It's a good job that Bruno picked up his scent and started barking. I was just about to light the fire.'

Mrs Johnson looked pale. 'What a clever dog,' she said gratefully. 'I'll have to think of a special treat for him. As for you,' she wagged a finger at Freddie, 'you will go straight back in your box. I'll make sure the shed door is tightly closed this time, just in case you fancy a walk again before spring.'

Helen giggled. 'We wondered if you would like to come and watch our fireworks, Mrs Johnson?' she asked.

Her neighbour beamed. 'I should love that, thank you. I haven't been to a Guy Fawkes party for years.'

'Well done, Bruno,' smiled Helen happily, giving her dog a goodnight pat. 'I think you have made yourself another friend.'

CATHERINE COURTNEY

Hannah Helps Out

What a miserable wet Saturday! Hannah looked out of the window at the rain. Surely there must be something she could do on a day like this!

'Can I help with the shopping?' she asked Mum.

'No, thanks,' said Mum. 'I did it all yesterday. I won't need to shop today.'

'If it dries up, I could help in the garden,' Hannah suggested.

'No chance today,' said Mum, 'it will be much too wet underfoot.'

'I know,' said Hannah, 'I'll go round to see Gran.' Hannah liked visiting Gran, who lived just round the corner.

There were lots of ways she could help gran.

So that afternoon she set off, carrying some little cakes Mum had just made and jumping over the puddles on her way. She rang Gran's bell but there was no reply. She peered through the window. There was no sign of Gran. Perhaps she is out shopping, thought Hannah, but she always shops in the morning.

Hannah rang the bell again.

Then an upstairs window was flung open and Gran's head popped out. 'Hello!' she called, 'down in a second.' Her face was streaked with dust and she wore a scarf round her head.

'I thought you must be out,' said Hannah when Gran opened the door.

'No,' said Gran, 'it was such a miserable day, I decided to clean out a cupboard I hadn't touched for ages. Just look at the dust!'

'I'll help you,' said Hannah, 'and here are some cakes Mum sent for your tea.'

'Oh, thank you,' said Gran, 'yes, I could do with some help.' Hannah put on one of Gran's big aprons and took a duster and they started to clean things out of the cupboard.

'Wait a moment!' said Gran. 'Just look – I haven't seen this for years.'

She dusted the cover of an old photograph album.

'See, that's me at school – and there's my best friend with the pigtails and that boy in the back row – he was the bad boy in the class.'

Hannah was fascinated. Surely this round-faced little girl wasn't Gran? 'That's me all right,' said Gran smiling.

After a bit, Gran said, 'Dear me, this isn't getting the cupboard cleared out. Now, let's see what else we've got – oh, look at these old magazines. Don't the fashions look odd!' Together Gran and Hannah heaved a big suitcase out of the cupboard. They gasped as the locks sprang open.

'My old dance frocks,' said Gran. 'Well, I never.'

'Isn't this beautiful?' said Hannah. She lifted out a pink dress trimmed with beads. 'Can I try it on?'

'Of course,' said Gran.

'And what's in that box?' asked Hannah.

'My old hats,' said Gran. 'I can't bear to throw them away.' She brought out a big white hat trimmed with flowers round the brim.

'That's the one you were wearing in the photo,' said Hannah.

'Yes,' laughed Gran, 'I thought I was ever so smart.'

'Can I try it on too? Don't look – it'll be a surprise . . .'

Hannah popped into Gran's bedroom and tried on the pink dress. Then she put on the hat. It came right down over her ears. Last of all, she put on a pair of silver shoes with pointed toes. It wasn't very easy to walk in them, so she held the pink dress up with both hands and shuffled back to Gran.

'Here I am,' she said.

Gran laughed and laughed, 'Who's under there?' she asked, mopping her eyes. 'Oh dear, I never saw anything so funny.' A little later on, when Hannah had tried on all the hats, Gran looked at the clock. 'My goodness – I don't know where the afternoon has gone to. Let's put all this back where it belongs and have a cup of tea and some of those cakes.'

'Put things back?' said Hannah.

'Yes, I'm not throwing out these treasures. Unless you'd like to borrow the pink dress and the white hat for the Brownie concert?'

'Oh, yes, please.' Hannah was delighted.

So they put all the cases and boxes back again and sat down to tea.

'Oh dear,' said Hannah. 'I haven't helped you clear out the cupboard. I meant it to be a Good Turn.'

'Never mind,' said Gran. 'I haven't had such a good laugh for a long time – and showing you all my old photos and treasures has done me good. It cheered me up a lot on a rainy day. So you have done a Good Turn after all!'

ANNE FORSYTH

The Almond Present

Lida lived in Denmark. One day Mum said to her: 'Lida, we're going to England to spend Christmas with Grandma.'

Lida knew Mum had come from England, but she, Lida, had never been there, so she was very excited. She told everyone she knew, and they all said how lucky she was, and what fun it would be. All, that is, except Pers who lived next door.

'Huh. You won't get your Almond Present for Christmas there,' he said.

'Of course I will,' said Lida. 'I always get it.'

'No you won't,' retorted Pers, who was a bit of a know-all. 'They don't have Almond Pudding in England, they're different, you see.'

This made Lida think hard, and rather sadly, too. She would miss her Almond Pudding and Present. Every Christmas Mum made a lovely pudding with cream and rice, almonds and other

delicious things. All the almonds were cut into very small pieces, except one. And if you found this one whole almond in your portion of pudding, then you had an extra present.

Up to last year Lida had always been the lucky one to find the whole almond in her pudding, but it looked as if this year she would not have it. She told her mother what Pers had said, and Mum said that Pers was right about Almond Puddings – they didn't have them in England at Christmas.

But Lida had no time for feeling sad in the busy days that followed. Not only was there packing to be done – Mum did most of that anyway – but most important of all they had to choose special presents for Grandma and lots of uncles and aunts and cousins Lida had scarcely met . . . and this time they would be taking the presents to them, not sending by post – so the choosing was really exciting.

Thus Lida did not think any more about the Almond Present until Christmas Day itself. For dinner they had turkey and chestnut stuffing, and suddenly Lida remembered – there would be no Almond Pudding! It just didn't feel right.

Then Grandma brought in a big round, brown pudding with a piece of holly stuck into the top of it. As she gave Lida her plate, she said: 'This is our Christmas Pudding, Lida. But eat it slowly.'

Grandma and Mum laughed, but Lida didn't feel like laughing one little bit – she thought again of the creamy-coloured Almond Pudding, and then she thought how black and peculiar the English one looked! But, of course, she was too polite to say so aloud.

'Eat up, Lida,' said Dad, and Lida looked at him reproachfully. Surely he knew how she felt – Dad was Danish, after all.

'Try just a little bit,' whispered Mum. So Lida picked up her spoon and tried – mmm, not too bad. She broke it up a little, and was about to take another piece onto her spoon when something bright gleamed up at her. It was shiny. What was it? She pushed the pudding aside and there, lying at the bottom of her dish, was a bright new coin.

Grandma and Mum were laughing again. 'I hoped you'd find it, Lida,' said Grandma. 'Sometimes we put new coins into our puddings for the lucky finders, sometimes we put in pretty charms. You have found the coin, so now you can buy whatever you like with that coin. It is yours, for an extra present.'

But Lida shook her head. 'I'm going to keep it,' she said. 'You see, it's an Almond Present, well almost, and I'm going to show it to Pers –

he was wrong. Christmas is just the same in England as in Denmark, isn't it, Mum?'

NANCY SCOTT

A Challenge from Uncle Bill

It was nearly the end of Pow-wow when Brown Owl said, 'You know my Uncle Bill?'

The Brownies nodded. Brown Owl's Uncle Bill was always full of ideas and had sometimes started the Brownies off on most unusual ventures.

'He's just been working with a touring acting company,' she went on. 'They're closing down now and are getting rid of the scenery and props. They were throwing these out,' she continued, pointing to a bulging sack, 'but Uncle Bill said he had a use for them . . . with Brownies.'

'You mean with us?' asked Julie.

'Yes, with us. Sixers, pull the sack over here and open it, will you.'

There was a moment's silence then:

'Whatever are they? Golly! I know . . . Clogs!'

Yes, clogs, large solid wooden clogs, each a good twelve inches long.

'But whatever are we supposed to do with

them?' asked Caroline, rather disappointed.

'Look, there's something in this one,' cried Jackie. 'It's a letter. She read:

'Dear Brownies,

Are you willing to lend your twelve pairs of hands by using these twelve clogs? We're running a bazaar for the Animal Shelter and want to have some original ideas. One way is to have an ABC Show, which is short for A Brownie Clog Show. Each Six can use their clogs in any way they like.

I do hope that you will help us.

With all best wishes

Uncle Bill'

'I don't see what he means,' wailed Julie.

'It's easy,' said Jackie of the Pixies. 'We just all *do* something with the clogs. You know, like putting earth in them and planting crocuses or something.'

'Sh!' said Margaret. 'Don't go giving away your ideas – we're going to need six if we all do it.'

'It's all right for you Pixies,' moaned Claire, Sixer of the Elves. 'You're always full of ideas but I don't know what on earth we're going to do.'

'Well, you'd better all go to your Six Corners and start to plan,' their Guider suggested. 'But remember, it must be something you can do without me: now we've no Tawny, so I shan't have time to give anyone much help.'

Ideas flowed quickly in the Pixies' Corner as everyone had expected, but there was also a steady hum of activity coming from the Elves as plans were made.

It was the third week when trouble started for the Elves.

Claire consulted her list. 'You, Jennifer, how's the lamp going?'

Jennifer's brother was learning to be an electrician and she had asked him if he could fix up her clog and make it into a bedside lamp.

'I'm frightfully sorry,' said Jennifer, nearly in tears. 'I'd almost finished making the shade and Roger was ever so careful, but something went wrong and he says he can't do it.'

'Oh well, we'll use the clog for something else.'

'We can't. It was nearly ready but the bulb was too hot or something and the clog's all burnt and spoilt.'

'Never mind,' said kind-hearted Julie. 'We've still got five.'

'Four,' said Paula grimly. 'My gran's thrown mine away.'

'Thrown it *away*?'

'Yes. She's sorry now, but I made her mad.'

'Why, what did you do?'

'Well, I was making a kind of hanging basket out of it, and I'd got the earth and plants and everything in it and I tried hanging it over the front door to see what it looked like.'

'What's wrong with that?' asked Jackie.

'Nothing – but, you see, I was watering it from the bathroom window, and how was I to know that Gran had asked one of her friends to tea?'

'Well . . . ?'

'Well, I suppose I hadn't tied it up all that firmly, 'cos just as the friend was going out, it sort of tipped and all the earth and stuff sloshed out on her hat. Gran was furious.'

Some of the Elves laughed, but not Claire. 'So we've just got the four now,' she murmured.

'Three,' whispered Susan, who had not yet spoken.

'Three?' gasped Claire. 'Don't say something's happened to yours?'

'No, nothing's happened: it's just lost.'

'Lost? You can't *lose* a clog.'

'No, I know, but Mum's in hospital and our Help keeps putting things away and I've asked

her and asked her and she can't remember what she's done with it. I've looked everywhere.'

'Well, you'd better go on looking,' said Claire glumly. 'Now what about the rest of you?'

The remaining Brownies seemed to be progressing fairly well, and, feeling rather scared, they went off to their homes determined that nothing should happen to their clogs.

But by the fourth week disaster had struck again.

'Mummy made me throw it away,' said Julie who had been trying to turn her clog into an aquarium. 'Some of the tadpoles turned into frogs and my sister trod on one and she screamed the roof off. Then Mum made me empty it in the pond, and it smelt awful and she wouldn't let me keep it.'

'And what about you?' asked Claire turning to Jackie.

'It didn't work. We tried your idea of putting a little clock in and then a stand at the back, but we must have gone wrong with the screws. It's all split and splintered now – what about your experiment?' she asked hurriedly.

Everyone looked hopefully at the Sixer. Claire flushed scarlet. 'It *was* working quite well,' she began. 'I'd got it to stand up and I'd fixed it so that it could be used as a photo frame and then, well, I was doing it in the garden.' She paused.

'What happened?'

'Mummy called me in, and you know the two puppies next door? Well, they must have got into the garden, and they always go for any sort of shoes . . . They chewed it to bits.'

The Six groaned, then Jackie spoke. 'That's the lot then – unless Susan finds hers.'

'I have found it.'

'You have?'

'Our Help suddenly remembered she'd put it on a shelf in the garage and so I rushed out and looked, and there it was, but I couldn't touch it.'

'Whyever not?'

'Because it's got a bird's nest in it, and eggs, and the mother's sitting on them.'

'Sitting on them in your clog? Gosh, how lovely!'

'Yes, but that doesn't help the Six!'

'Oh yes it does,' yelled Claire. 'Quick, I've got an idea. Listen.'

The Elves crowded round their Sixer . . .

'What on earth's "A Brownie Clog Show"?' asked puzzled visitors making their way round the Animal Shelter Bazaar.

Out of curiosity they put their entrance fee into the clever clog money-box the Pixies had made with a cheery Dutchman's face painted on it.

The small boys rushed to Vicky's stall for she was calling out, 'Try a clogful of home-made sweets at ten pence a time.' And she was kept busy measuring out the sweets which all the Six had helped to make.

Some of the older visitors made their way to Caroline. Her clog was full of small posies and button-holes. As soon as they were sold, she filled it up again with a fresh supply.

Then came Emma's clever model depicting The Old Woman Who Lived in a Shoe. The old lady, a carefully dressed doll, looked in horror at all her pipe-cleaner 'children' scrambling over their clog home. The youngest visitors spent their time rushing from this to Premila's exhibit which was a doll's cradle. Her mother had helped her to make a beautiful muslin cover, while her brother had fitted rockers on the bottom of the clog.

Finally there was Rachel's clog full of mustard and cress, and by it, pieces of flannel cut in the shape of clogs all covered in mustard and cress seeds for sale for five pence each.

Then the visitors streamed on to the Elves' Show.

First they saw the large piece of card on which

Jennifer had written this verse:

Come this way and you will see
How a robin and her babies three
Found a home safe from cat and dog
Because they nested in a clog.

At the home of a Brownie Elf,
In a garage on a shelf,
Someone put this clog away
And then forgot it by next day.

The anxious bird this fine clog found
And laid her eggs all safe and sound.
Now they're hatched and flying free –
The mother and her babies three.

From this an arrow pointed to THE ROBIN MUSEUM.

In a place of honour stood the clog, still with its small well-shaped nest inside. By it were drawings of the male, female and baby birds and the eggs. In a note book nearby was a carefully written story of the clog babies. Some visitors pored over this while others tried the competition.

On a table were collected all kinds of things which birds might use for building their nests: twigs, straw, feathers, moss, sheep's wool, mud, grass. The competitors had to see who could build the best nest from any of these materials.

In one corner were some Christmas cards, all featuring robins, which had been painted by Jackie, the Pack artist. In another Jennifer was selling 'Robins' Eggs' – little pink marzipan sweets with grey flecks in them.

Uncle Bill was delighted with the ABC Show. So was Miss Edwards, the bird specialist of the Animal Shelter. She spent an extra long time in the Robin Museum, then said, 'Congratulations to you all. I had no idea that this was the kind of thing that Brownies did.'

‘Perhaps you would like to come and visit the Pack and tell them more about birds,’ suggested Brown Owl. ‘We love having visitors.’

‘And I love talking about birds,’ said Miss Edwards, ‘so that’s a deal. Thank you very much.’

‘And *perhaps*,’ said Claire as she looked happily at her Six, ‘perhaps as well as helping Uncle Bill to collect money for the Animal Shelter, we may have helped ourselves to collect a new Tawny Owl!’

AILSA BRAMBLEBY

Jenny's Christmas Present

Jenny stood in the kitchen talking to her mum. That afternoon she was visiting an old people's home with her Brownie Pack.

'Shall I take something for the tea, Mum?' asked Jenny. 'Brown Owl said we could if we liked.'

'What about some biscuits and I'll give you some mince pies as well.'

'Thanks,' said Jenny. 'Can I take some chocolate biscuits too?'

Mum smiled. 'All right, but mind you don't scoff the lot. It's for the old folks, remember.'

On Saturday afternoon, Jenny met the rest of the Brownies outside the rest home. They were shown into a large lounge, where people sat around in comfy chairs, watching television, reading newspapers and playing card games. Jenny looked around with interest, wondering what it would be like to live there.

There was a Christmas Tree in one corner,

and a few decorations but the big room looked rather bare and sad.

The Brownies sang carols and had tea. Then Brown Owl persuaded everyone to join in some Brownie songs.

Jenny and her friends handed round the food, then chatted to some of the old people. They were all kind and very interested in the Brownies.

On the way home Jenny found herself thinking about the rest home, and wondered if they had pretty decorations for their own private rooms. It would be awfully miserable if they didn't.

When Jenny arrived home, Mum asked her all about the visit.

'We had a great time. They loved our cakes and the chocolate biscuits!' grinned Jenny. 'But the house wasn't Christmassy, not like at home.'

'Well maybe they haven't many decorations. They cost a lot of money and I expect most of the ladies and gentlemen don't feel like making things,' replied Mum.

'That's a pity. I wonder if my Pack could do something.' Jenny looked thoughtful.

'Ask Brown Owl; she may have a few ideas,' suggested Mum.

So, at the next meeting, Jenny approached Brown Owl with her plan.

CAROLS

‘I see what you mean, maybe you could make something bright for the entrance hall?’ said Brown Owl.

‘I’d like them to have something pretty for their own bedrooms though, to make them feel nice and happy for Christmas,’ replied Jenny.

Brown Owl smiled. ‘That’s a bit ambitious, but if you come up with anything you’re welcome to try. Why not have a think with some of your friends?’

That night, as Jenny lay snuggled in her warm bed, she thought hard. It was a cold wintry night, frost was already turning the trees silver under the clear starry sky.

At last Jenny fell asleep, thinking about silver trees and frost. The next morning she awoke with a start.

‘That’s it, I’ve got it . . .’

Dressing quickly she ran downstairs to tell Mum.

‘Hi love, you’re up bright and early for Sunday. Fancy some slightly lumpy porridge?’ smiled Mum.

‘Mum, I’ve had a brilliant idea for the decorations,’ shouted Jenny.

‘Have you? And what is it?’

‘I’m not going to tell you yet because I don’t know how they’ll turn out. It will be a surprise.’

Mum laughed. 'OK, I think I can wait.' Jenny grinned back at her, but wouldn't say anything else.

In the morning she went for a walk in the nearby woods with some of her Brownie friends and a couple of their elder sisters. The woods were still and quiet in the cold air. But everyone was too busy gathering small branches and twigs to notice the freezing weather.

They came back with arms filled with fallen branches and spent a busy few hours in Jenny's garage. Now and again Jenny would appear and rummage through the kitchen and hall cupboards for 'things'.

Mum left them to it, intrigued and amused by their frantic activity. At teatime she knocked on the garage doors.

'Are you frozen in there? Come into the kitchen for hot crumpets and tea, you must all be starving by now.'

Jenny called out from inside. 'Nearly finished, show you in a moment.'

A few minutes later Mum heard laughter and chattering. Jenny and her friends appeared carrying their afternoon's work.

'Let me look. How pretty,' praised Mum. 'You have done well.'

The Brownies had painted the branches white,

then stuck them into little yoghurt pots, and decorated them with little bows, tinsel, washed milk bottle tops and tiny wrapped boxes. Each branch was now a miniature, frosted Christmas Tree.

The Brownies showed the rest of the Pack the trees at the next meeting.

'That's a great idea, girls, we'll take them along on Saturday. How many have you managed to make?' asked Brown Owl.

‘Fifteen,’ replied Jenny, ‘will that be enough?’

‘I think so, but I’ll check for you,’ said Brown Owl.

The following Saturday Jenny and the other Brownies took the little trees along to the old people’s home.

They were delighted, and each person had one sitting on their window ledge, where it caught the light and shimmered, to give out a real festive feeling.

JUDY F. TAYLOR

Pippa of the Pixies

'It isn't *fair*!' said Pippa, defiantly. 'Why should I leave my friends, and school, and Brown Owl, because of Dad's job? I'm not going!'

'For the thousandth time, Philippa,' said her mum wearily, 'it's not up to you. Dad's been transferred to Manchester; we go next month. There's no point in making a fuss.'

Pippa scowled and kicked the carpet. Looking at her, nobody would imagine she was a nice girl. She felt like being grumpy, and that was what she was going to be!

The worst thing about moving from London was leaving her Pack. Pippa was sure there wasn't anyone like Brown Owl in the whole world, and besides, at Christmas she would have become the Kelpies' Second. It was the worst possible time to go. Pippa already hated Manchester, where she knew everyone talked strangely. She probably wouldn't understand a word they said.

At Pippa's last meeting, Brown Owl gave her a furry owl as a goodbye present. Pippa cried as she left, hugging the owl close, and cried most of the way to Manchester, till her exasperated mum gave her a good talking to.

'You're just wet,' remarked her brother as Pippa sat sullenly, giving the occasional sniff. 'I think it's an adventure, going somewhere new. And it's only for one year.'

'*A year!*' muttered Pippa, sulkily. It sounded so long.

Pippa was surprised to find their new house was nice. Set in a pleasant suburb, it had red-brick walls, slate roof and a big lawn. Pippa's bedroom was small but pretty and her pink bed-spread matched the wallpaper exactly. She'd expected the North to be dark and smoky like the Lowry paintings her mother liked. This was quite different and she felt better.

School wasn't bad. Pippa made friends with Emily and Sarah, who sat near her. They had a peculiar way of talking but she understood them and quite enjoyed herself.

'You do talk funny, don't you?' said Sarah one day, quite kindly. Pippa prepared to argue but Emily got in first.

'She's from London,' she told Sarah. 'They all talk like that down there. They say barth for

bath and things like that.' She turned to Pippa and smiled. 'Don't worry, you'll soon learn to talk like us. It isn't hard.'

Pippa was so astonished that Emily thought she'd *want* to speak like them that she didn't say a word!

When Pippa had been up North for two days, she had a visitor; a young lady, who announced she'd come to invite Pippa to Brownies. She was so different from her London Brown Owl that Pippa said so before she gave herself time to think! Pippa's mum tutted but the lady laughed.

'That's all right! Brown Owls come in all shapes and sizes,' she said. 'Come and meet Tawny and Snowy on Wednesday and see how *they* look! We've a place in the Pixies; sorry you can't be a Kelpie; we don't have Kelpies in our Pack.'

'How did you know I was a Kelpie?' said Pippa, astonished. 'Have you seen my uniform?'

Brown Owl smiled. 'We have our methods,' she said, mysteriously. 'I also know that you've just passed your Road, have five Interest Badges and your Brownie birthday is February 15.'

Pippa gasped. It seemed like magic. She thought she might like this new Pack after all.

She did. Tawny and Snowy were just as nice as Brown Owl and the Brownies were really friendly. Her Sixer and Second, Jill and Elizabeth, said they were glad to have her, because the only three Pixies were all only seven, and a nine-year-old was just what the Six needed.

Snowy, in charge of Highway, was pleased to have Pippa, too, because four of the five Highway Brownies were going to Guides at Christmas and Emily needed a partner. Altogether Pippa was made to feel very welcome and suddenly the move to Manchester didn't seem quite so bad.

Time flew, and soon it was Christmas. Pippa had a part in the Pack pantomime and

thoroughly enjoyed herself. Then she had a big surprise!

At the first January meeting, Brown Owl announced the names of the new Sixers and Seconds. Pippa had secretly hoped that she just *might* be the Pixies' Second but her mum had warned her that as she'd only been in the Pack one term, it probably wouldn't happen. But Jill and Elizabeth had both gone to Guides, so there *might* just be a chance . . .

What was Brown Owl saying? Had she heard right?

'Pixies' Second . . . Lucy; and Sixer . . . Pippa. Congratulations!'

Not Second! Sixer! Pippa could hardly believe it and had never felt so proud.

The oddest thing was that a year later, when Pippa's dad was offered the chance to stay up North instead of returning to London, it was Pippa who begged him to accept. Michael wanted to go back to his favourite football team; Mum missed her friends and the Oxford Street shops, and Dad couldn't make up his mind!

'*Dad!*' said Pippa, urgently. 'Please don't move! I can't leave all my friends, and school, and Brown Owl. Please, Dad! It isn't *fair*!!'

Which is where we came in.

GILLIAN ELLIS

The Chickenpox Camp

'I don't know why you're so miserable today,' sighed Paula's mother wearily. 'It's a lovely sunny day and you're on holiday from school. Why don't you go out and play instead of moping around indoors with such a long face?

'I hope you're not sickening for something,' she remarked, feeling her daughter's forehead. She did feel rather warm . . .

Paula wiped her eyes crossly. 'I just feel really *horrible*,' she said.

'Perhaps you'd better go and have a lie down on your bed, then,' suggested her mother, and to her amazement Paula agreed.

She fell asleep almost at once and when she woke up it was lunchtime. For a while she lay listening to the sounds of other children playing outside, and wondering why she had been asleep at such a strange time. Her head ached and she felt hot and uncomfortable. She rubbed crossly at an itchy place on her tummy, then another one on her back. The itchiness didn't stop, so she pulled up her t-shirt to have a look.

'Mum!!!' It was more of a scream than a shout. Paula's mother nearly dropped the teapot she was holding, and raced up the stairs at once.

'Chickenpox!' she announced as soon as she took a look at the spots all over Paula's tummy.

'Never mind; I'll put some lotion on those spots to stop them itching quite so much. You'll soon be better.'

'How soon?' asked Paula, her eyes brimming with tears. Her mother looked at her sadly. She knew she would have to tell Paula the truth, but she was going to be disappointed.

'It looks as though you'll have to miss Pack Holiday.'

It was late in the evening by the time Mrs Davies phoned Brown Owl to tell her the news. Paula had been feverish and irritable all day, and her mother had spent most of her time sitting with her, playing games and reading her stories, but nothing would take her mind off the Pack Holiday she was going to miss.

'She'd been so looking forward to it!' she explained to Brown Owl. 'It's such bad luck. It would have been her last holiday as she'll be a Guide next year.'

'What a shame!' agreed Brown Owl. 'She's not

the only one. Mary's got chickenpox too, so she won't be able to come either.'

Mrs Davies thought for a moment. 'You've just given me an idea!' she exclaimed. 'I wonder if Paula will agree . . .'

Next morning, Paula was covered in spots from head to toe and felt more miserable than ever. Every time she thought about all the other Brownies going off to their holiday home, she wanted to cry. It was so unfair! She was in no mood to be cheered up by her mother's idea.

'Mary's one of the little ones!' she sniffed, 'I hardly even know her!'

'It would help to cheer her up as well,' pointed out her mother. 'She must be just as disappointed as you are; it would have been her first Pack Holiday.'

'Well – it would have been my *last* one!' replied Paula, and turned away from her mother sulkily. Mrs Davies decided it would be better not to argue.

It wasn't until the afternoon of the next day that Paula suddenly announced, 'I feel better! Can I have some egg and chips? And can Suzie come round?' Suzie was one of Paula's special friends. She was a little older than Paula and was already a Guide.

Her mother laughed. 'I'm glad you're feeling

better, dear, but you certainly can't ask Suzie round! You're still covered in spots and very infectious! Why don't you phone her up and have a chat, instead?'

She was busy in the kitchen as Paula talked to her friend on the phone, but couldn't help overhearing her say, 'What? – you, too? Oh! So have I! Yes – spots all over! I bet I caught it from you! Oh, Suzie, I've got a terrific idea! Well . . . it was my mum's idea, really. Listen; you know Mary, who's just made her Promise . . .'

Mary's mother sounded very pleased when Mrs Davies phoned her to explain the plan. 'Mary's hardly stopped crying since she got the spots,' she said, 'She's so upset about the holiday. Are you sure it won't be too much trouble? – I know it will cheer her up!'

A few days later when they were all feeling much better, two spotty Brownies and one spotty Guide had their first *real* camp, in a *real* tent in Paula's living room! They also had another unexpected guest – Paula's little brother James, who had suddenly come out in spots the day before! 'You can join in with us, as you're not well,' Paula had said, feeling quite sorry for him for once. 'But only if you're quiet and don't tease anybody!'

First Paula's father cooked their tea – beefbur-

gers, sausages and bacon – over a real camp fire in the garden. Suzie helped, as she had learnt to do some outdoor cooking. Then Paula was allowed to have a try too and decided the sausage she cooked herself definitely tasted best! They washed up their own plates in bowls of water in the garden and then sang songs around the bonfire until it began to feel chilly outside. Then they all climbed into sleeping bags and squeezed together into the little tent indoors.

When Suzie's and Mary's mothers came to collect their daughters the next day, the tent and sleeping bags had all been packed tidily away and the house showed no signs of having been used as a Pack Holiday home!

'We'll have something to tell the rest of the Pack about, now!' Paula said to Mary as she was leaving.

'Yes!' replied Mary excitedly. 'I bet they'll all wish *they* had been to a Chickenpox Camp!'

SHEILA NORTON

Get Well Soon

All the Brownies were looking forward to the holiday, but Karen most of all.

'I've never been to the country,' she said. 'Fancy staying on a farm!'

'You can watch the cows being milked,' said Brown Owl, 'and maybe feed the hens, and collect the eggs . . .'

Karen's eyes opened wide. 'I can hardly wait.'

'My uncle's got a farm,' said Sally. 'I like feeding the pigs and watching the sheep dog working . . .'

Brown Owl smiled, 'You'll have a great time.'

The Brownies couldn't stop talking about the holiday, and Karen hopped and skipped all the way home from the Pack meeting.

'Can I do anything to help?' Karen asked. She had only recently made her Promise and she was determined to keep it by doing a Good Turn every day.

'Yes, please,' said Mum. 'Could you pop these letters in the box for me?'

Karen ran up the street to the pillar box – but she didn't notice the uneven paving stone.

'Oh!' she tripped and fell heavily.

'Are you all right?' A woman with a small dog stopped and helped Karen to her feet. 'Have you hurt yourself?'

'Ow . . .' Karen tried hard not to cry. Brownies were brave. They didn't cry but her ankle really hurt very badly. 'I can't stand on my foot,' she said.

'Where do you live?' asked the woman.

'At number seven – just along the street.'

'I'll help you home then,' said the woman. 'Put your arm round my neck.' So they managed to get back to Karen's house, even though she was limping badly.

'Karen's hurt her ankle,' Brown Owl told the Pack at the next meeting. 'So she won't be along this week or next.'

'Will she be able to come on the holiday?' they all wanted to know.

'Oh yes,' said Brown Owl cheerfully, 'she'll be fit enough by then but she's feeling rather miserable and lonely just at the moment.'

The Brownies decided they'd do what they could to cheer up Karen. They'd visit her and write letters and do funny get well cards.

'You know,' said Sally, after a moment, 'she'll miss all the excitement before the holiday.' That evening the Brownies were planning what to take with them on holiday and how long the journey would take and how much money they would need.

'I've got a very good idea!' said Sally. She explained to the rest of the Brownies what she'd just thought of.

'That's great!' said Brown Owl. 'I'm sure that will cheer Karen a lot and she won't feel so left out of things.'

'I'll write a poem,' said Laura, who was good at writing poems.

Karen really was feeling low when Sally and Laura popped in to see her. She tried to smile all the same and wanted to know all they had done at the meeting.

'These are to cheer you up,' said Sally, handing over an envelope. 'Don't open them till we've gone.'

What could be in the envelope? Karen was longing to look. When her friends had gone home, she opened the envelope. Inside she found a whole batch of puzzles, just like the ones in her favourite magazine. Then she noticed the poem.

> Do the puzzles one by one.
> Get well soon to share the fun.

The first puzzles meant joining up dots. Karen reached for a pencil. She began joining the dots. One, two, three, four . . . The first was a cow, the second a horse. Then there was a sheep dog. 'All the animals we'll see at the farm!' she said to herself.

Next there were a lot of jumbled letters. 'You will need these . . .' said the heading in big letters.

Karen began to puzzle out the jumbled letters. AKNROA – what could that be? 'Anorak!' she said. 'Of course, I'll need an anorak on the holiday!'

She started to work out the rest: ROUSTERS then YMNOE – and so on till she had a complete list of all the things she'd need to take.

The last puzzle showed a Brownie in the middle of the picture, wearing a huge smile. 'Get well soon!' said the heading and round it was a maze. Karen traced the puzzle with her pencil until she'd reached the smiling face in the middle.

Mum opened the door. 'It's teatime. Well, you do look cheerful!'

'Look!' said Karen. 'These are the best get well cards ever – what a terrific surprise!'

ANNE FORSYTH

Christmas Just As it Should Be

It was Christmas Eve and in their Scottish village the Brownies had a special job to do. 'I'm glad you can all help,' said Brown Owl. 'We must clean the big Nativity models and set them out on the village green. Then everyone in the village can enjoy them.'

The models really were big. They had been stored in Farmer McPherson's cellar and they were very dusty. The Brownies collected their dusters and began to wipe the plaster models clean. Fiona, the youngest Brownie, counted them. 'There's Mary and Joseph – and the baby Jesus in a little manger,' she said. 'Here are the shepherds and the three wise men – but where are the animals?'

'The animal models were damaged a long time ago,' said Brown Owl. 'I'm afraid there aren't any left.'

'But there should be!' said Fiona. 'Jesus was

born in a stable and there were animals nearby.' She looked upset.

'I know,' she said, 'we can go to Farmer McPherson and ask him for another manger – a big one, full of hay. That would remind everyone about the animals, wouldn't it?'

Farmer McPherson nodded when the Brownies told him what they wanted. 'Oh yes,' he said, 'I have a manger. It's a big one too. I'll carry it to the green and you can bring the bundles of hay.'

So, Farmer McPherson helped the Brownies set out the Nativity scene. Fiona carefully laid the baby Jesus in the tiny manger. Mary and Joseph were placed on each side and behind them stood the shepherds and the three wise men.

'We'll put the animals' manger at the back,' said Farmer McPherson. He looked up at the dark hills around the village and rubbed his hands. 'It's going to be a very cold night,' he said. 'I think it's going to snow.'

He was right. It was a bitterly cold night. The Brownies were snug and warm in their beds but up on the hills the animals shivered in their sleep. Snowflakes swirled among the trees and when morning came the ground was white.

The forest deer were cold and hungry. Their

leader knew that down in the village there would be food. Slowly and carefully he led his small herd through the trees and down the steep hillside towards the village. Sniffing the air, he led the way past the first cottages and there, in the distance, he saw food: a long manger full of hay. He looked round cautiously. There were some strange figures nearby but they would not hurt the deer. Calling softly to his herd, he went forward.

When the villagers woke up that Christmas morning they were surprised and delighted.

'Why,' they said to each other, 'look at the deer! Animals round our Nativity scene. Just as it was – and just as it should be.'

Farmer McPherson stood at his farm gate. He looked up at the big white hills – and then at the deer, quietly munching by the big manger. 'Happy Christmas, deer,' he said. 'Just as it was.'

Fiona looked out of her bedroom window. 'Happy Christmas, everyone,' she whispered. 'Just as it should be!'

JEAN HILTON

Pennies for Our Thoughts

Mr Brown looked up from his paper at his daughter, Sarah, who was lying back in an armchair, with her eyes shut and a frown wrinkling her forehead.

'Penny for your thoughts,' he said.

Sarah opened her eyes and grinned. 'You'd be wasting your money.'

'Maybe, but thoughts *can* be very valuable.'

'Pity our Pack can't buy some. You see, we've been asked to help at the SAVE THE CHILDREN garden party and we're absolutely stuck over what to do – and that's what I was thinking about.'

'Do you mean to tell me that all you Brownies haven't an idea between you?'

'Of course we've ideas – dozens and dozens of them – but either they're stale as anything or they're dull as ditchwater or someone's already doing them. What we want is something really different, something that has never been thought of before.'

'Mm, well, that's not so easy. Anyway, why not sleep on it: perhaps you'll have some ideas by morning.'

As Sarah lay in bed, nine words kept beating through her brain: 'Penny for your thoughts: thoughts can be very valuable . . . Penny for your thoughts: thoughts can be very valuable . . . Penny for . . .' but Sarah was asleep.

The moment Sarah woke up she knew she had the idea that was needed. It was maddening to have to wait for the Pack meeting and for Pow-wow but at last she could tell the others.

The Brownies were thrilled, but their Guider was doubtful.

'You'll never be able to manage it – not for a whole afternoon.'

''Course we will,' exclaimed Bridget and Susan, who with Sarah made up the Pack's three Sixers.

'And Brown Owl, we want to do it all by ourselves,' stated Melanie, one of the youngest.

'Except for the costumes, and getting the tent. We'll want your help with those,' said Susan.

'Well, I'm still not quite sure . . . how many of you want to do it?'

All fifteen Brownies gave the Pack sign.

Their Guider laughed. 'That's settled it then,' she said.

By three o'clock on the day of the fête which was held in a field behind Lady Beverley's house, a crowd was listening to the Mayoress as she spoke about the SAVE THE CHILDREN FUND. No sooner had she finished than all the people were thronging the stalls and side-shows.

Walking purposefully among them were Janet, Julie and Sally from the Gnomes, Kelpies and Sprites, acting as sandwich-board men. On their boards was written:

Pennies for our thoughts!
Do you need some ideas?
Have you any problems?
Come to the Brownie Guide Thinking Tent.
Five pence for each thought.
Money back if not satisfied!

Outside the Thinking Tent sat Sarah and Sandra with a spare chair between them. They were dressed as professors in long black gowns and mortar-boards. Inside, were the five Brownies who had to produce the answers. The rest of the Pack were having their turn to see round the fête.

'Sit up quick,' hissed Sandra. 'Someone's coming.'

It was Lady Beverley herself, whom everyone knew was a little vague. The Brownies brought forward the spare chair for her.

'You sell ideas?' she asked.

The Brownies nodded, terrified now that they were being put to the test.

'It's for my goddaughter,' went on Lady Beverley. 'It's her birthday next week and I haven't any idea what to give her for a present. I really know very little about nine-year-olds.'

Sarah and Sandra began to breathe again: this seemed a possible problem.

'What's she like?' asked Sandra. 'Energetic, or more the "sit-down-and-read" type?'

'Oh energetic. Very energetic indeed.'

Sarah stood up. 'I will go and discuss with the Thinkers,' she said.

She burst into the tent so hurriedly that her mortar-board hat was knocked off.

'Quick,' she said. 'Think of a good present for a nine-year-old girl who is energetic. Philippa, you should know: you've got your Athlete's badge.'

'Rich or poor?' asked Fiona.

'Well, it's Lady Beverley and I suppose you'd call her rich.'

'Pogo stick, roller skates or skateboard,' said Philippa promptly. 'All on sale at Boyce's.'

Sarah stuck on her hat and went out again.

'Our Thinkers suggest a pogo stick, roller skates or a skateboard,' she said.

'Roller skates? Skateboard? I'd never have thought of these. Have you any idea where I could buy them?'

'Yes, Boyce's.'

'Oh, Boyce's. Yes, a very reliable firm. Well, my dears, you've given me good ideas *and* told me where to buy them so you've answered two questions.'

'Hurray! Ten pence for our first go,' said Sarah. 'Oh, I say, Miss James from the library is coming: surely she knows everything.'

A minute later Miss James was sitting on the question chair.

'Now,' she said, 'I'm very anxious to find a really good recipe for gooseberry jam.'

Sandra looked blankly at Sarah. 'I'll go and consult our Thinkers,' she said gloomily.

She went in to the waiting Brownies. 'Gooseberry jam,' she said mournfully. 'Someone wants a recipe.'

'You ought to know,' said Philippa to Maria. 'You've got Cook's Badge.'

'I didn't make jam, silly.'

Fiona jumped up. 'I know!' she exclaimed. 'Ask her to come back in ten minutes.'

As Sandra returned to the front of the tent, Fiona crawled under the brailing at the back and rushed to the Home-Made Stall run by the Mothers Union.

'Mrs Barber,' she panted. 'Please, you make gorgeous gooseberry jam. Please could you tell me your recipe; it's ever so important.'

Mrs Barber laughed. 'Why the hurry? All right, dear, if you've a pencil, I'll jot it down for you.'

After the ten minutes, when Miss James returned, she was handed the piece of paper.

She looked very puzzled. 'Now how on earth did you know that recipe?'

'We didn't exactly know it,' confessed Sandra, 'We got it from Mrs Barber of the Mothers Union.'

Miss James burst out laughing. 'That serves me right,' she said. 'I wanted to see if I could catch you out, but you've caught me. Mrs Barber is my sister and that's an old recipe of my mother's which we've both used for years.'

Sandra looked blank. 'I suppose you'd like your money back?'

'Certainly not. I asked you a question and you produced a very good answer. I'm going to recommend you and send you some more clients.'

She must have done for soon they had a stream of visitors. Then in a brief lull their Guider came to see how they were getting on.

'Marvellously,' said Sandra. 'The rector's been to ask where he could find the Plant Stall. The Mayoress wanted us to think of a way to keep her bouquet fresh – that was easy: Maria borrowed an empty jar from the Flower Stall. One mother asked if we'd find her Bobby's kite. We sent a message to the sandwich-board Brownies to keep a look-out and they found it. Then there have been lots and lots of people wanting help with their parcels.'

'Good, well I think it is time you changed over jobs now,' said their Guider whose work it was to sort out the turns.

'Let's keep our eyes open,' suggested Sarah, as she and Sandra went off to visit the stalls. 'Then we might see something that would help us with an answer later on.'

An hour later, when their Guider told them it was time to stop business, the Brownies reeled off the jobs they had done:

'We've drawn a map . . .'

'. . . to show the way to the church.'

'We've stopped Billy Brown's nose bleeding.'

'. . . he'd been hit by a coconut.'

'And we've fixed up his little sister's pants for her . . .'

'. . . you see the elastic had gone . . .'

'And . . .'

'Just a minute,' interrupted Brown Owl. 'Is everyone here? We've got a new problem – one that really does need some thought. It's the Mayoress. She's lost her handbag.'

'Gosh,' said Julie, 'I expect it's got lots of money in it.'

'No. She said she wouldn't mind having lost the bag. What's really bothering her is that the notes for her speech this evening are in it.'

'What does it look like?'

'It's smallish, cream in colour, with handles.'

'Oh, I know,' said Sarah. 'I've seen it. Sandra, remember? The Mayoress had it hanging on her arm when she was having a go at bobbing corks in the water.'

'That's right, and it got in her way . . .'

'Yes, and she took it off her arm and put it on Miss Jones's Household Stall, among the tea towels.'

'But every stall-holder has searched for it,' said their Guider.

'Tea towels,' said Bridget thoughtfully. 'You know, I've seen a tea towel somewhere else today. Oh yes, on Mrs Hornby's basket . . . You know, that old lady who's half blind.'

'That's nothing,' said Julie. 'She always carries that basket and she always puts a tea towel on top when she's bought any food. It's one of her fads: she's got a thing about germs.'

'Yes,' agreed Bridget, 'but it looked different somehow. Oh do *think*, someone. Didn't anyone else see her?'

'I saw her, I saw her,' squeaked Melanie, '*and* she was near the bobbing cork thing when the Mayoress was having her go. And she was making a fuss of Miss Jones's Labrador puppy and she put her basket down to pat him, and he was jumping about all over the place.'

But no one had seen any more.

Perhaps it was because Sarah understood puppies, or perhaps it was because she had been working out ideas all afternoon – she never knew which – she suddenly had her brain-wave.

She looked at Brown Owl and said slowly, 'I think that handbag is in Mrs Hornby's basket.'

'Oh no, Sarah,' protested Brown Owl. 'She's the most honest soul in the world.'

'Oh I didn't mean she took it. Listen,' she went on quickly, 'the handbag was on the tea towels on the stall. Mrs Hornby's basket was on the ground near the stall. Couldn't that puppy have pulled at the towel, tugged it down so that the bag fell in the basket and the towel on top of it?'

'Well . . . it's a bit of a wild guess on your part, Sarah, but I suppose it is just possible. Anyway, let's find Mrs Hornby.'

'You won't,' said Julie, 'I saw her going home about half an hour ago.'

'Then we'll go after her.'

Mrs Hornby did not live far away and it was not long before the Brownies returned from the cottage, and in their hands was – the handbag!

'Good thing we went,' said Melanie. 'Did you hear what she said? She said she wasn't going to unpack her basket until she had had her tea and that would have been miles too late for the speech.'

The Mayoress was most relieved and checked at once that her notes were safe.

'Brownies, I'm very grateful,' she said. 'This last job must have needed dozens of thoughts, so here's a fifty pence piece to cover them all.'

'Golly,' exclaimed Melanie, 'that ought to help them to save lots of children!'

Sarah said nothing but she was thinking, 'Well, Dad was right; thoughts certainly can be valuable.'

AILSA BRAMBLEBY

Castle Adventure

The Brownies climbed off the coach, chattering eagerly to each other.

'Do you think we'll see the Queen?' asked Jenny.

'Or Princess Diana?' added Katy.

'I don't think so,' replied Miss Gordon, their Guider. 'The Royal Standard isn't flying. That means that the Queen isn't staying here.'

The two Brownies were disappointed. Ever since the Pack had planned this trip to Windsor Castle, they had been hoping that they might see the Queen.

'What's the Royal Standard?' asked Anne.

'It's the Queen's flag and it flies over any building she's staying at,' Miss Gordon explained. 'Come on, Brownies, hurry up or we'll never get to see anything.'

The Brownies lined up in twos and walked up the hill towards the castle's main gate. They stopped to watch a soldier outside a sentry box.

He looked very smart in his bright red jacket and black bearskin hat.

Kim decided to take a photo and was thrilled when the guard stood to attention as she clicked the camera.

'Thank you,' she called as she went inside the castle grounds with the rest of the Pack.

'What do you want to see first?' asked Miss Gordon, looking at a sign post.

'The doll's house, please!' cried most of the Brownies.

They followed the path which led them to the doll's house entrance. Miss Gordon paid for the tickets and the Brownies joined the long queue of tourists waiting to go into the building.

The Brownies were very excited as they slowly made their way inside a small, dark room. There, in front of them, stood a huge doll's house.

Katy and Jenny pressed their faces to the glass and gazed at the rooms, each fitted with tiny furniture.

Suddenly there was a rustling sound and Jenny turned to see a man in a blue cagoule push his way through the crowd.

'Hey, wait your turn!' cried a few people

But the man ignored them and continued pushing, until he stood in front of the two Brownies.

He muttered something under his breath about 'kids being a nuisance' and then started pushing through the crowd again.

'Ouch!' shouted Katy as he trod on her foot. The man didn't hear her and made his way through the crowds of people until he reached the exit door. Katy stared after him angrily.

'What a rude man,' she said. 'He really hurt my foot.'

'Never mind,' comforted Jenny. 'He's gone now. Come on, let's look at the rest of the house.'

A short while later, when the Pack was gathered in the open air, Miss Gordon gave a shout of dismay. 'My purse, it's gone!'

'Perhaps you dropped it while we were looking at the doll's house,' suggested Anne. 'Shall we go and look?'

Miss Gordon left the Brownies with Mrs Grey, Tawny Owl, while she and Anne went to find the purse.

They came out a short while later shaking their heads. Miss Gordon's purse was still missing.

'Apparently,' said Miss Gordon, 'several people have reported lost belongings this morning. There must be a pickpocket about.'

The Brownies felt sorry for their Guider and offered to lend her their pocket money. Miss

Gordon refused all their offers and decided that the best thing they could all do was enjoy the rest of the outing.

At lunchtime the Brownies walked to the river to have a picnic. After her sandwich box had been emptied, Katy took off her shoe and sock to examine her foot. Jenny bent over to have a look too. A large, purplish bruise was developing.

'Ouch,' said Jenny. 'That must hurt!'

'It does,' replied Katy. 'What a horrible man he was. He didn't even apologise.'

Just then Jenny had a thought.

'Katy, don't you think he was acting strangely?' she said.

'What do you mean?'

'Well, pushing through the crowds without looking at the doll's house and wearing a cagoule when it wasn't raining.'

'I suppose so. But perhaps he wore it because he was cold.'

'Or because it had big pockets,' said Jenny.

'Big pockets?'

'Yes, big enough to put things in.' Jenny was getting quite excited.

'Don't you see, Katy, he could be the pick-pocket!'

The two Brownies didn't have time to discuss

their idea, for just then Miss Gordon called them to pack up their bags ready for a boat trip down the river.

The boat trip made all the Brownies forget about their Guider's purse. They had a lovely time and were disappointed when the trip ended.

On the way back to the castle to catch the coach home, Jenny suddenly pulled Katy's arm.

'Look over there,' she whispered and pointed towards a man walking in front of them. He was wearing a blue cagoule.

'That's the man who stamped on my foot!' shouted Katy. Then she stopped. 'Look, Jenny!' she exclaimed.

The two girls watched in amazement as the man walked past an old lady and took a purse from her bag. He put the purse into his pocket.

'Quick,' yelled Katy, 'we must tell someone.'

They ran up the road, completely ignoring their Guider who was calling them back. Ahead of them were a couple of policemen. The two Brownies caught up with them and quickly told them about the man in the blue cagoule.

One policeman followed the man while the other took Katy and Jenny back to the Pack. He explained to an angry Miss Gordon what had happened.

The Brownies watched as the man was arrested and taken to a nearby police car.

The policeman thanked the Brownies for using their sharp eyes and told Miss Gordon that he hoped they would find her purse. He wished the Brownies a pleasant trip home and went to join his friend in the police car.

Then the coach arrived and the Brownies climbed on, talking about the exciting end to the outing. As they left Windsor the Pack gave Katy and Jenny three cheers.

The two Brownies sank down in their seats,

tired out after the day's events.

'What an exciting day,' murmured Jenny and with a small sigh she fell asleep.

LYNN HURDWELL

Beccy Wins Through

One day Beccy came home from school looking very upset. She used to enjoy school but now she hated it and often woke up in the mornings wishing she was ill.

Mum looked at her with a worried frown on her face. 'What's wrong love?' she asked.

'Nothing,' Beccy replied.

Mum put an arm round her. 'Tell me. I know you're not very happy at the moment.'

Beccy turned to Mum, and said quietly, 'I can't do the work properly at school and some of the other girls call me stupid.' Beccy ended in a rush and sat closer to Mum.

Mum frowned. 'That's not very kind, tell me more.'

Now Beccy started telling Mum and all her worries came tumbling out.

'When I'm reading the letters look all fuzzy, sort of mixed up and funny,' she explained.

'I see, so you can't make out the words clearly, is that it?'

'Yes, I think so,' Beccy replied.

Mum gave her a huge cuddle. 'Don't worry. I'll go and see your teacher.'

'All right,' Beccy said sadly, really worried.

'Quick, it's nearly time for Brownies. Run and change.'

Beccy bit her lip. She didn't even want to go to Brownies any more in case people laughed at her.

'I don't want to go tonight, Mum.'

'But you've finished your Collector badge. Come on.'

'My tummy hurts,' Beccy pretended.

Mum smiled gently. 'I'll tell Brown Owl you're not feeling too brave at the moment. Will that help?'

'S'pose so,' Beccy said half-heartedly. She used to love going to Brownies but was so afraid she'd have to do some hard writing or read something out.

Mum had a word with Brown Owl, who was a very kind person and also a teacher.

She had a quiet word with Beccy while the other Brownies were busy.

'Beccy, your mum explained that you're unhappy at school. Try not to worry about things.'

'I can't do things properly,' Beccy said sadly.

'But you've collected a lovely lot of postcards for your badge and you made a super cake the other week.'

Beccy nodded but still felt confused. She couldn't understand why she couldn't read or write easily when she tried really hard all the time.

Her best friend Clair came over. 'Done the homework for Miss Jacks?'

'No, not yet,' Beccy said.

'I'll help you; it's easy peasy,' Clair said.

Clair was the only one who didn't say mean things when Beccy got stuck with her work.

The next week, Mum went to see Miss Jacks and Beccy couldn't wait to hear what had happened.

'She's very friendly,' Mum began. 'We had a long chat and looked at your work and the reading books.'

'I like her too,' Beccy said.

'Well, she thinks you may be dyslexic.'

'What's that? Is it bad?' Beccy asked.

Mum laughed. 'No, it just means that you can't read the words easily, a sort of word blindness, so you'll be having some extra help which in time will make things much easier.'

At Mum's words Beccy felt much happier. 'So I'm not stupid after all?'

‘No, of course not, you’re not to worry any more and I’ll tell Brown Owl at the next Pack meeting,’ Mum said.

At school the next day, Miss Jacks spoke to Beccy kindly. ‘I’m very sorry you’ve been upset. We’ll work through some easier books together in class and then another special teacher will be seeing you too.’

‘Will I be able to read quickly like Clair soon?’ Beccy asked.

Miss Jacks smiled. ‘It’s not easy being dyslexic but it’s also a problem that can be got round with the right help.’

That day at school was one of the happiest for Beccy. Now she understood what had been wrong, and that she wasn’t stupid at all.

At the next Brownie meeting she had another happy evening. Brown Owl came over to her and said: ‘SNAP, Beccy.’ Then she started to laugh.

Beccy was puzzled. ‘What do you mean Brown Owl?’ she asked, surprised.

‘I’m dyslexic as well, Beccy,’ Brown Owl told her.

Beccy gasped, really amazed. ‘You are too?’

‘Yes, thousands of children and grown-ups are and they get along very well.’

‘But you can read and write and everything,’ Beccy began.

'I can now but I often got stuck and have learned ways of getting round it,' Brown Owl explained.

Beccy gazed at her Brown Owl in amazement. It seemed strange that such a big grown-up could also have trouble like her.

'I've some good news for you too,' Brown Owl went on. 'I've sent your Collector badge entry for a County competition; it was very good.'

Beccy grinned happily. Now her world seemed straighter. She felt better inside and would definitely not want to miss Brownie meetings ever again.

JUDY F. TAYLOR

The Unexpected Bridesmaid

Holly was small for her age. She had dark curly hair and a few freckles. She was also upset and angry. Her friend Sophie was having a party next Saturday and had invited all the Brownies except Holly. That's what it felt like anyway.

'Why has she left me out? I'm always friendly to Sophie,' cried Holly.

'Perhaps she forgot. It can happen,' suggested Mum.

'No. She gave out all the invitations while I was there. She saw me. She would have said something if she had just forgotten. She just doesn't like me any more.' Holly sighed. 'It's because I've got freckles.'

'Of course it's not, Holly. Freckles are just right with your colouring. You'll be very glad of them one day.'

But Holly still felt like being mean. She wouldn't play with her little brother when he got out the Lego. She wouldn't help Mum dry the dishes after lunch and she wouldn't help Dad wash the car like she usually did on Sunday mornings.

It was the school holidays and by Wednesday Mum threatened that if she didn't cheer up there would be no outings, no treats, not even a visit to Granny.

Granny lived in the next town and had planned to come over on the bus for the day. But she rang up to say she had fallen over and sprained her ankle and couldn't come. Holly was very fond of Granny and was sorry she wasn't well. So she decided to make some cakes to cheer her up: Mum said they would go over to see Granny instead.

As Granny couldn't walk just now, she asked Holly to go to the shops for her. They were very near and there were no roads to cross. She gave her a list; just bread, some stamps and cotton wool from the chemist.

In the chemist Holly was surprised to see her teacher, Miss Bennett. Miss Bennett was getting married on Saturday. 'A spring bride,' Mum had said. 'How romantic.' 'Yes,' said Holly, 'she's having two bridesmaids and a pageboy.'

'I don't know what to do now,' Miss Bennett was telling the lady chemist, 'now that my niece has caught chickenpox, and very badly too. I'm a bridesmaid short. I really am sorry for Lauren, she's as disappointed as I am, but I had so set my heart on two dark-haired bridesmaids.'

Just then Miss Bennett glanced round and saw Holly.

'Why, hello, Holly. Fancy seeing you here.'

'Hello, Miss Bennett. I'm visiting my granny. She's not well and I'm doing the shopping,' Holly said proudly.

Miss Bennett looked closely at Holly, measuring her with her eye, her height, her dark hair . . .

'Holly, you're a sensible girl. Are you doing anything special on Saturday?'

'No, Miss Bennett.' The birthday party she had not been invited to sprang immediately into her head.

'Could I come back with you and talk to your mother?'

Over a cup of tea Miss Bennett explained her situation to them. 'So you see, Holly is exactly the right size for the bridesmaid's dress. My poor niece is so spotty, and feels so unwell that there's no way she can come to the wedding. Could Holly? Would Holly?'

'Please, Mum!' begged Holly.

It was a wonderful day. The sun shone and Holly did everything she had practised in the

rehearsal the day before. The dress was a dream. Holly's dress that is. It was pale blue, covered in bows and frills and the hairdresser had done her hair in a special way with rosebuds and curls. She carried a posy of spring flowers.

The photographer took so many photographs that Holly felt she would fidget if he took just one more. But she was given a large one of herself in all her finery and one of the bride and groom with the bridesmaids and pageboy.

She was not allowed to keep the dress. Miss Bennett, or rather Mrs Jackson as she was now, explained to her that her niece would so love to have the dress, and as it had been made for her, would Holly mind if she gave it back at the end of the day?

'Of course. I quite understand,' Holly said. 'I've had a wonderful day. I've always longed to be a bridesmaid and I'll have the photograph to remind me. Thank you, Miss Bennett, I mean Mrs Jackson, for asking me.'

'I'm glad now I wasn't invited to Sophie's party,' Holly confided to Mum as she munched her way through a slice of wedding cake.

DIANE CHORLEY

Fat Fred

The Brownies were playing Barnyard Bedlam, yelling as loud as they could, and didn't notice the scratching at first. Then Joanna heard it. Just a tiny sound. She listened hard . . . there it was again, near the door. Scratch, scratch . . . then another sound, quite different. A sad little whimper.

'I think we have a visitor,' smiled Brown Owl, going to the door. Soon she was back, cuddling a small brown dog. The Brownies crowded round, patting and stroking; the little scrap wagged its tail furiously, giving short, excited barks. Rather odd to look at, with large floppy ears, pot-belly and long feathery tail, it wasn't at all pretty, but somehow appealing. It wore no collar.

'It must be a stray! Could we keep him, Brown Owl?' asked Joanna, eyes shining. She'd wanted a dog as long as she could remember. 'He's *beautiful*. Look at his lovely eyes.' The dog ran to Joanna and licked her cheek appreciatively, exactly as if it knew what she'd said. Brown Owl shook her head.

'No, Jo, of course not! It probably isn't even lost. It's well cared for and well-fed . . . see that fat tum! The owner's bound to be looking for it. I'll put it outside again.'

'But it's *lost*!' chorused the Brownies.

'It'll soon find its own way home, don't worry!' said Brown Owl.

But Brown Owl was wrong. When she shut the door, the scratching immediately began again, accompanied by a mournful howling. At seven-thirty, the dog was still there, and when Joanna started for home, it trotted happily behind her.

'Who's your friend?' said Dad, meeting her at the corner.

'Oh, Dad!' said Joanna, breathlessly. 'It's lost. Can we take it home, just till it's claimed?'

'OK,' said Dad, smiling at Jo's excitement. 'But no fuss when it goes. Promise?'

'I promise,' beamed Joanna, and she skipped all the way home, the dog frisking at her heels.

Mum raised her eyebrows as the little dog hurtled round the garden. At suppertime, Joanna brought the panting animal into the kitchen, and her mother looked at it critically.

'Not a raving beauty,' she observed, putting down some water. 'Now then, Fred, what shall

we do with you?' Joanna giggled.

'You can't call him *Fred*!' she said, but her mother disagreed.

'He *looks* like a Fred,' she insisted. 'And that's what *I* shall call him . . . till he's claimed,' she added hastily. Dad came into the kitchen.

'The police say no one's reported a lost dog,' he told Joanna, who couldn't help feeling pleased. 'But it's early days. I expect we'll find the owner before bedtime.'

'Can I stay up and play with it?' asked Joanna quickly. 'If I promise to get up the minute you call me in the morning?'

'Till nine and not a second later,' said her mother firmly.

By nine, no one had phoned; Mum gave Jo a grocery box and an old blanket, and helped her settle Fred in the kitchen. Joanna awoke next morning feeling excited; at first she couldn't remember why, then it all flooded back. She ran to the kitchen and with great relief, saw Fred, still there, tail wagging eagerly. He scampered over and jumped up, licking Joanna in delighted welcome.

Jo didn't want to go to school; she was worried that Fred would be claimed during the day. At hometime, she flew back and rushed into the kitchen. Fred was gone.

Joanna burst into tears.

'It's not fair!' she sobbed. 'I wanted to keep Fred. I love him.'

'Hey!' said her mother, giving her a hug and a tissue. 'Stop crying, and I'll tell you something nice.' Joanna wiped her eyes and blew her nose noisily.

'A lady came for the dog this morning,' said Mum. 'She only missed it very late last night.' Joanna's eyes filled again.

'So he's gone?'

'Well, no,' said her mother. 'Oddly enough, Fred's still here.'

Joanna jumped up, excited.

'Didn't the lady want him?' she said. 'Can we keep him?'

'Not exactly!' laughed her mother. 'But by the time Fred's owner got here, Fred was busy. Come and see.'

Joanna's mother led her into the hall. There in the alcove under the stairs lay Fred, proud as Punch, surrounded by six squirming pups. Joanna gasped.

'Fred's a *girl!*' she whispered in astonishment. 'No wonder he was so fat!' Fred wagged her tail and gave the pups a motherly lick. Joanna's mum pulled her away.

'Leave them alone for a few days,' she said.

'Then we'll have a closer look. Just let Fred get used to them first.'

Joanna was so thrilled she hardly knew where to put herself. She couldn't understand why Dad put his head in his hands and groaned when he heard the news.

'That's all I need!' she heard him mutter. 'My front hall turned into a Maternity Home!'

Joanna rushed into Brownies next week to tell everyone about the puppies. Brown Owl reacted much as Dad had done.

'Whatever will you *do* with them all?' she said. 'I told you to take no notice of that dog last week. I'm sure she'd have gone home if you hadn't encouraged her.'

Joanna told the Guiders that her dad was taking Fred's new family home at the weekend, because their real owner wanted them.

'Won't you miss them?' said Tawny, sympathetically.

'Yes, I will' said Joanna, biting her lip. 'But the lady says I can visit Fred whenever I want.'

The owner was as good as her word. When Fred and family were back in their real home, she suggested that Dad brought Jo round after Brownies every week to play with the pups. It wasn't the same as having them all the time, but it was better than nothing. Joanna enjoyed watching the pups grow and loved the visits.

One Tuesday, instead of the tumbling pups at the door, there was only Fred. Her owner explained that she'd spent the evening delivering the pups to their new homes. Joanna stayed a while to play with Fred, but she missed the pups terribly and it wasn't the same. Soon Dad called for her.

'Come on, Jo, Mum's waiting. Let's get back.' Joanna followed him to the car, her heart heavy, and they drove home.

'I shall never see the puppies again,' she said sadly and a big tear trickled onto her uniform.

Joanna had hardly put her foot inside the hall when a bundle of brown fur hurled itself into her arms. A rough little tongue licked frantically at her face and scrabbling paws sent her Brownie Handbook flying. Mum laughed at Jo's astonished expression.

'Yes, Jo, she's yours!' she told her. 'I hope we chose the right one?'

'My favourite!' exclaimed Joanna, quite overcome. 'The one with the smudge under its chin, just like Fred!' To her own surprise, she began to cry again.

'Only this time it's because I'm so happy!' she explained, watching the puppy scamper into the kitchen, fat little legs slithering on the tiles.

'You must think of a name for her, Jo,' said Dad. 'A *girl's* name . . . let's get it right this time!'

'How about Freda?' suggested Mum, grinning, and Joanna giggled.

'Freda's the Promise Elephant!' she said. 'I can't call her after an elephant! Anyway, I know a much better name!'

'What's that?' asked her father.

'*Brownie*, of course,' said Joanna.

GILLIAN ELLIS

The Brownie Who Was Scared of the Dark

Kirsty had always been frightened of the dark, ever since she could remember. She had her glow-worm, George, but still begged her mum to leave a light on.

'I know it's babyish,' she told her friend, 'and I *have* tried. But I keep imagining horrid things. D'you think I'm silly?'

''Course not!' said Debbie, loyally. 'My mum screams if she sees a mouse, and Dad hates injections. Your scary thing's different, that's all.'

'But *you're* not frightened of anything,' said Kirsty, enviously. Debbie grinned.

'Oh yes, I am!' she declared. 'School rice pudding!' And Kirsty giggled, thinking how lucky she was to have a friend like Debbie.

In May Kirsty's Brownies went on Pack Holiday, way out in the country. The girls were thrilled.

'It's so *different* from home!' said Debbie. 'So fresh and clean!'

The first day was exciting! So much to explore, so much to do. Time flew, and soon eighteen weary Brownies were climbing into their bunk beds.

'You can talk till nine,' Brown Owl told them. 'Then I want you all to be quiet and get to sleep as soon as possible. We've a busy day ahead tomorrow.'

Kirsty was glad that talking had to stop at nine, because it would still be light enough to see, and she badly wanted to be asleep before dark. George was a great comfort, of course, and she was relieved to see that several other Brownies had glow-worms, too; but it was the first night Kirsty had ever spent away from home, and the dormitory door was shut tight. The light from the Leaders' room was only just visible, a thin ribbon under the door.

Kirsty tossed and turned, unable to sleep. She longed for peace and quiet, but some of the others were not obeying Brown Owl. There were whispers and giggles, then someone had the bright idea of flashing her torch at the ceiling. Suddenly the room was alive with torch beams, as others joined in, and the muffled giggles became uncontrollable laughter. The door open suddenly and a very cross Brown Owl made her feelings clear.

'Not one word more!' she said sternly, collecting all the torches. 'You'll be worn out tomorrow at this rate! Off to sleep, please!'

The girls settled down, and Brown Owl went away. Soon Kirsty could hear regular breathing all around her and realised she was the only one still awake. It was totally dark.

'It's terribly quiet here,' thought Kirsty nervously. 'I didn't realise how many noises there are at home . . . cars, planes, people talking, the TV downstairs . . . I don't think I like the country after all.'

Kirsty had never noticed before how the street lamp outside her house lit up the bedroom. Here the world outside was completely black and silent; even George didn't help much. Kirsty could hear her own heart thudding in the stillness. Suddenly an animal's shriek rent the air, followed by the eerie hoot of an owl, and Kirsty gave a little squeal. A moment later Brown Owl tiptoed quietly into the room, and came over to Kirsty's bed.

'Still awake?' she whispered. Kirsty tried to be brave, but two big tears trickled down and plopped onto Brown Owl's shirt.

'It's too quiet,' she sniffed, 'and . . . and too *dark!* I didn't want to say, because I know it's stupid, but I can't help it. I'm afraid of the dark.'

Brown Owl hugged her.

'There's really nothing to fear, Kirsty,' she said. 'It's a beautiful night, but there isn't much of a moon, so it's extra dark. Tell you what, hop out of bed and I'll show you something lovely. Wrap up well and come with me.'

'Where to?' said Kirsty, struggling into her trainers.

'Ssssh!' said Brown Owl, and taking her hand, she led Kirsty through the front door to the verandah.

'Look up!' whispered Brown Owl.

The black sky was spangled with sparkling jewels and Kirsty gasped in delight. She had never seen the stars like this before; the town lights made the night sky misty and spoiled its beauty, and the buildings got in the way.

'It's like velvet!' Kirsty murmured softly. 'And the stars are like diamonds! They're *gorgeous!*' Brown Owl pointed out different groups of stars.

'They all have names,' she explained. 'Great Bear and Little Bear, Orion, Cassiopeia, Gemini . . . and lots more. A friendly sky, wouldn't you say, with all those people and animals in it . . . ?'

'Where do the stars go in daytime?' asked Kirsty.

'They're right there, all the time,' answered Brown Owl. 'But it has to be dark for us to see them.'

'So night-time does us a favour,' said Kirsty, thoughtfully. 'Or we'd never see the stars?'

'That's right,' agreed Brown Owl. 'There's no need to be afraid of the dark; though, of course, you'd never go outside alone at night – that could be dangerous. But it looks lovely from inside.' Kirsty yawned, and Brown Owl took her hand.

'Back to bed?' she suggested; and suddenly

Kirsty knew it would be all right now. George would be beside her and she wouldn't be afraid any more, with all those friendly stars twinkling at her through the bedroom window.

GILLIAN ELLIS

Just a Piece of String

'Six box inspection today,' called out Alison, Sixer of the Gnomes. 'Hope you've all brought something.'

Mary, newest member of the Pack, looked anxiously at the little piles being built up in front of the Brownies as they emptied their pockets. There were note books, clean hankies, pencils, odd coins, a compass, a bandage and even a piece of bubble gum.

'You'd better put that away quick,' advised Alison. Then she looked at the empty space in front of Mary. 'Haven't you got *anything*?' she asked.

Mary opened the hand she had been clenching and said in a low voice, 'Just a piece of string.'

'Oh well, that's something. It doesn't matter. You're new after all.'

But to Mary it did matter. She longed to do something for her Six, the Gnomes, but they all seemed so big and so clever . . .

‘Quick, stand up!’ cried Alison. ‘Here’s Brown Owl.’

The Guider looked at the Gnomes’ piles and then stopped in front of Mary.

Alison spoke up quickly. ‘It’s because she’s new, Brown Owl. All she’s got is a piece of string, but she’ll have more next week.’

‘Just a piece of string,’ repeated Brown Owl thoughtfully. ‘That’s a very good thing to start your collection with. String can be used in all sorts of ways.’ She turned to the rest of the Pack. ‘Brownies, here’s a challenge for you. By next week see how many uses you can think of for string – any kind of string, long or short, thick or thin, and we’ll see which Six has the longest list.’

All the way home Mary tried to think of uses for string and even when she was in bed. As she lay there, half asleep, she fiddled with her piece of string, twisting it and knotting it until, to her surprise, she found she had made it into the shape of a little man. She put it on her pillow and shut her eyes.

‘Come along, come along, if you want to find out our uses.’

Mary sat up quickly. It must have been her String Man talking to her. But how he had grown! He was now about half as big as she was.

'Slip into your clothes and then we'll be off,' he added.

'B-but we can't go out now,' stammered Mary as she struggled into a t-shirt and jeans. 'We'll wake up my family.'

'Not if we go by the window. *My* family will help us. Here, catch this.'

Just in time Mary stretched out her hands and caught the ball of string the little man had thrown to her.

'Good thing you didn't drop it.'

'Why?' asked Mary. 'I could easily have picked it up again.'

'Oh no you couldn't. That's my Family Call-Up Ball, but once you drop it, it won't work for you any more.'

'What do you mean?'

'That's enough questions. Now let's see. We'll need a strong fellow for this: you'd better call up one of my uncles.'

'Me? How?' asked Mary.

'Use the ball of course. For an uncle you must unwind the string while counting to eight.'

Mary began to count and unwind the ball at the same time. 'One, two, three . . .'

'That's right, that's right, but steady now: don't drop it.'

'. . . six, seven, eight. Oh,' cried Mary, and she very nearly did drop the ball as over the window-sill twirled what looked like two great snakes.

'Don't worry, don't worry. It's only Uncle Rope. He's made himself into a ladder for us. Come along, down we climb.'

As they reached the ground, Mary gazed at the ladder as it slid away and disappeared into the bushes.

'Now hurry up, hurry up or we'll miss the night shift at the factory,' urged String Man.

'The factory?' queried Mary. 'What factory?'

'The one where the String Family learn their jobs, of course.'

'But where's the factory?' cried Mary. 'I can only see a door.'

'Don't fuss about details,' replied String Man. 'All in good time. Now then, unwind six for one of my cord brothers.'

Counting to six, Mary unwound carefully.

'Right, now ring the bell.'

'Ring the bell? What bell?'

'Use your eyes, use your eyes. Can't you see Brother Cord?'

'Oh, yes,' exclaimed Mary and put out her hand to tug at the bell-pull which had appeared by the door.

Without a sound, slowly, very slowly the

massive door opened.

'Thank you, Brother Cord,' said String Man. 'Now then, get a move on so that I can show you all the works. No need to wipe your feet – the whole floor's covered with string matting.'

'But what works?' asked Mary as she gazed round her, for she could see nothing but plain walls and one door.

'Goodness, what a one you are for questions! My family's works, of course. All the different kinds of jobs done by my relations – close ones and distant ones. You've no idea what an enormous family we String People are. Now, let's see. I think we'll call on my nephews and nieces first. Naturally they are only youngsters so they are just learning the simpler jobs – there are plenty of those. Four unwinds for them, please.'

Excitedly Mary began to unwind the ball.

'Steady, steady,' warned String Man. 'You know what I said about dropping that ball.'

Going more slowly, Mary counted to four.

The door opened. Mary gasped.

All round a vast room were pieces of string – on the floor, in the air, on tables, and every piece was busy on some job. One was winding itself round a parcel, another round a yo-yo. One was tying up a balloon and another whipping a coloured wooden top. Others were working string puppets, weaving themselves into shopping-bags, and even knotting themselves into hammocks.

'These are the beginners,' said String Man. 'The next stage is the Sports Centre. Come and see.'

Mary followed him and saw string used on netball posts, string on the handles of cricket bats and string being made into tennis and football nets.

Suddenly String Man strode across to another corner. 'Now then, now then,' he said sternly, 'that's not what you are here for!' He pounced upon two pieces of string having fun trying out all kinds of 'Cat's Cradle'. 'Back to work, you two.'

'Of course, they're very young,' explained String Man to Mary, 'so you can't blame them for playing about now and again. But we'd better move on.' He led the way to another door.

'Three unwinds for the teenagers, please. They're on the next floor.'

Mary counted to three. The door opened, showing a staircase. They climbed up to the next floor and entered the next part of the factory.

Here they saw some sturdier members of the String Family, different kinds of cord, all busily at work. One was fixing itself onto wooden handles and becoming a skipping rope. Another was twisting round two poles to make a clothesline.

'Wrong knot,' called out String Man. 'You need a round turn and two half hitches there.'

One piece of cord was winding round a frame to make a fireside stool while another was fixed as a lead onto a dog's collar.

'What's over there?' asked Mary, pointing to a far corner.

'Ah, that's the Camping Department. Guy ropes for tents, lifelines for swimmers, and good strong cord for tying up bedding rolls; you'll need them all when you're a Guide. But come along, we're off to see the grown-ups now. Ten unwinds for them. Where's your ball? Don't say you've dropped it?'

'No, I've still got it,' replied Mary as she counted to ten.

Through the door and up the stairs they went, to a room at the top of the building.

'Why,' gasped Mary, 'these are all like your Uncle Rope who made the ladder for us.'

'That's right, but keep your voice down. These are elderly, experienced workers with responsible jobs and they don't like to be disturbed. Their work is often a matter of life and death.'

'Life and death?' queried Mary.

‘Come round and I’ll show you. Now that one is to pull great liners out of docks. Think what would happen if they broke. These are a bit thinner but mountaineers and pot-holers will use them so they must be of top quality . . . and so must these which are for tethering bulls or hauling cars, and look at that sturdy one in the corner. He’s for ringing huge church bells weighing a ton or more. Look, he’s going to have a practice now . . . 1, 2, 3, 4, 5, 6. Six o’clock in the morning it is. Make haste, make haste, time you were back at home.’

Mary started for the stairs.

‘Not that way, not that way,’ directed String Man. It will be quicker by the roof. Follow me. The steps are steep but there’s a good rope handle to hold on to.’

Through a trap door they went, onto a flat roof.

‘On board, on board,’ cried String Man, pointing to a shiny red helicopter, with propeller already moving.

As Mary scrambled in awkwardly the ball of string slipped out of her hand, rolled along the roof and over the edge. ‘Oh well,’ she said to herself, ‘we probably don’t need it any longer . . .’

But they did. The helicopter began to lurch, twist, bump and quiver.

‘Where’s the ball?’ shrieked String Man.

‘I’ve dropped it,’ said Mary, ‘but I thought it wouldn’t matter now.’

‘Not matter? Not matter indeed? Here we are in a crashing helicopter and you say it doesn’t matter . . . ?’

Mary went very white.

‘Don’t dither, don’t dither!’ cried String Man in his most hustling tone. ‘You’ve got your parachute on so what are you waiting for? Jump out, count ten and pull the cord.’

Mary shut her eyes, jumped, counted and then pulled the cord. As she heard a great rustling sound above her she dared to open her eyes.

Hurray! her parachute was working. It billowed out above her like an enormous umbrella.

Down, down, down, softly, softly, softly she glided . . . so gently that she never knew when the parachute had landed nor did she know how she had found her way back into bed.

But where was String Man? Thank goodness, there he was, safe on her pillow, and, strange to say, he was quite small again.

It was Pack meeting once more.

‘Now I wonder how many of you remembered the string challenge?’ asked Brown Owl. ‘Sixers, you write down all the ideas your Sixes can produce.'

Alison of the Gnomes took out her book. 'We'll hear yours first, Mary, as you're the youngest.'

Mary started off: 'Rope ladder, bell-pull, mats, string bags, washing lines . . .'

'Hey, wait a minute, I can't keep up,' wailed Alison.

Mary paused for a few moments and then went on: 'Whips for tops, tennis nets, fishing lines, skipping ropes, fireside stools . . .'

'Stop, stop!' cried Alison. 'We must give the others a chance.'

Each of the Gnomes gave a few ideas and then it was Mary's turn again. 'Guy ropes, lifelines, dog leads . . .' On and on she went.

'Haven't you Gnomes finished yet?' asked Brown Owl.

'No,' said Mary, 'I've lots more.'

'Well you can have another minute and then you really will have to stop.'

'Right,' said Mary. 'Ropes for towing cars, ropes for mountaineers and pot-holers, bell ropes, cords for parachutes . . .'

'Time's up. Sixers, bring me your papers.

'Why, Gnomes,' the Guider said a few moments later. 'Your list is longer than all the others put together. However did you do it?'

'It was Mary,' cried the Gnomes. 'She's String Champion of our Six.'

'And of the Pack as well,' said their Guider with a laugh. 'And to think that it all started with your piece of string!'

AILSA BRAMBLEBY